AND GOD SAID,
"LET'S BABEL"

AND GOD SAID, "LET'S BABEL"

The Bible As Cross-Cultural Communication

PHILIP McCARTY

iUniverse, Inc.
Bloomington

And God Said, "Let's Babel"
The Bible As Cross-Cultural Communication

iUniverse books may be ordered through booksellers or by contacting:

iUniverse
1663 Liberty Drive
Bloomington, IN 47403
www.iuniverse.com
1-800-Authors (1-800-288-4677)

ISBN: 978-1-4759-6558-2 (sc)
ISBN: 978-1-4759-6559-9 (hc)
ISBN: 978-1-4759-6560-5 (e)

Library of Congress Control Number: 2012922827

Printed in the United States of America

iUniverse rev. date: 12/27/2012

Other Books by Philip McCarty

God: A Self-Portrait

All the Way from Kingdom Come: Basic Future Events

To Mom and Dad

CONTENTS

INTRODUCTION

For the Christians are distinguished from other men neither by country, nor language, nor the customs which they observe. For they neither inhabit cities of their own, nor employ a peculiar form of speech, nor lead a life which is marked out by any singularity ... But, inhabiting Greek as well as barbarian cities, according as the lot of each of them has determined, and following the customs of the natives in respect to clothing, food, and the rest of their ordinary conduct, they display to us their wonderful and confessedly striking method of life.
—Epistle to Diognetus, chapter 5

IN THE BEGINNING, GOD spoke the universe into existence. It was an act that created a method of communication, as all nature speaks to us about God. When God created humans, he believed it was imperative that they have the capacity to communicate. God created various languages at Babel, and over time each language became the root of a culture. Today, the biblical name Babel is associated with communicating in different languages and, by extension, various cultures. So if God were to say, "Let's Babel," it would mean that he desires to communicate with people of every language and culture.

One definition of *culture* is "the ideas, customs, skills, arts, etc., of a people or group that are transferred, communicated, or passed along ... to succeeding generations."[1] Culture, therefore, involves more than just language; it includes the way people think and view the world. With that in mind, this book considers a culture to be any group that has a similar way of looking at the world—whether poor, oppressed, or disabled; rich, powerful, or able-bodied.

The passage from the Epistle to Diognetus quoted above asserts a truth that was viable in the second century and is still so today: Christians are spread throughout the populated world, speaking many languages and living in a variety of cultures. Since the beginning of the church, this is the way it was intended to be, so that the Gospel of Jesus might reach every tribe, tongue, and nation. God desires to speak to all people through the Bible, not just the people of the church.

The ideal method of interpreting the Bible stirs great debate among theologians, seminarians, and intellectuals. Some people believe that their method is the only true one. Usually average people are not very concerned with these debates; they just want to know how to understand the Bible. While there are different and viable methods, no single method has the monopoly on how to obtain meaning. In fact, the Bible deserves a method that is not culturally centered, but instead can adjust to all cultures. There is, however, something that can be gained from each method.

I am not advocating that all the methods of interpretation are equally valid. What I propose is that any valid method has to conform to established standards of human communication and have appropriate theological boundaries. Human communication is cross-cultural, yet each culture has specific ways of interacting within its own group. Both aspects of communication must be taken into account in any method of interpreting the Bible. However, some methods are simply wrong and yield results that are harmful to the scriptures and to the interpreter. In other words, interpretation does matter because some boundaries should not be crossed. In this book, we will delve into what transcultural hermeneutics look like and how they work.

By quoting from others throughout the book, I also will show that the interpretation of the Bible cannot to be confined to an individual culture. We live in a multicultural world, and God desires to speak to each and every group in a culturally relevant and understandable way. God loves the entire world, not just a particular culture within it. The church, the body of Christ on Earth, is composed of multiple cultures. When you are finished with this book, I hope that you will understand that no single culture has all the answers or can dictate the constitution of the global church. You do not have to be a member of a particular culture for God to communicate with you through the Bible.

This leads me to my core reason for writing this book. I asked myself if God is really concerned about me, my culture, my circumstances. The answer is a resounding yes! Each individual is important enough for God to want to communicate directly with him or her through the written words of the Bible. Throughout the Bible, we see God speaking to large populations and to individuals. God is a very personal God and wants to communicate personally with everyone. Depending on our cultures, we communicate with each other in different ways. God understands this and allowed for it when he created the Bible.

Why is it important to understand the Bible as a cross-cultural text? That is the first thing I asked myself before starting this project. I have read many books on how to interpret the Bible. I have read perspectives on the Bible from various cultures. I have not read a book, however, that examines the Bible as a cross-cultural book. Maybe it is not that important? On the contrary, how people view the Bible relates directly to their view of God and themselves. That makes this topic very important.

Understanding the Bible as cross-cultural keeps it from being chained to ancient Judaism or first-century Christianity. In other words, it helps us recognize that the Bible was not just for certain cultures or periods of time. God cares about people in all periods of history, including the present. We must not think that, because no books of the Bible are being written today, God cares less about the people of our time than he did about the ancient Jews or early Christians. If we simply see the Bible as a 2,000- to 3,500-year-old book, then it will not have an impact on our lives today. God still wants to be part of our lives and to speak to us just as much as he wanted to speak to the Bible's original writers and readers.

The Bible has the ability to speak to all cultures, including yours and mine. It is as relevant to the cultures of today as it was to the ancient cultures of Judaism and first-century Christianity. To keep God chained in the past makes him irrelevant to our lives today. God does not just belong to the past; he is the God of the present. We, as modern individuals and cultures, are important to God, and God's presence is with us.

I hope this point will come through as you read this book. Rather than having a single chapter listing authors from various cultures that I've found through my research, I refer to them throughout the book. I believe this gives them the legitimacy they deserve. I hope that by reading their quotations you will see that God does speak cross-culturally, and that we can learn from each other.

To me, this idea of the cross-cultural Bible is very important, particularly today, when the world has so many different and changing cultures. That is especially true for countries like the United States where so many cultures live side by side. More important, it is imperative for everyone to understand that the cross-cultural Bible is able to speak to you in your culture. This makes it a living and relevant book throughout time and not one that is confined to a particular period or culture.

To be honest, I had not thought about the Bible as cross-cultural until a few years ago; and I had never heard the topic addressed in school or from the pulpit. The truth began to hit me during a seminary class on cross-cultural communication and was confirmed when I read a portion of Donald K. Smith's book on Christian communication.[2] The only other books that seem to come close to touching the topic are those that promote culturally based hermeneutics. Yet I have come to believe this idea is very important to each individual. If God does not care about your culture, then God does not want to communicate with you in a way you can understand. Why would you want a relationship with that kind of God? His depth of commitment to a relationship with you is shown through the Bible's cross-cultural text.

This book will show that the Bible is indeed a cross-cultural document, how that affects the church as a whole, and what it means to individuals. My desire is that this book will help us change as individuals. I have taught the Bible for more than twenty-five years, received a BA in Bible studies and one in religious education from Tennessee Temple University, and completed an MA in Christian thought at Bethel Seminary. You would think I'd have it all figured out by now, but the more I've studied this topic, the more it has changed my life. I became confident in the knowledge that God cares about me as an individual who lives in a culture that was unknown to biblical writers. It has helped me recognize the church for what it is—a transcultural organism within the various cultures on the earth—and see my place within it. It has deepened my love for people from other cultures. I pray that you will begin to understand how much God cares for you as an individual and that God wants to communicate with you, no matter who you are.

SECTION I: THE BIBLE

Chapter 1:
The Cross-Cultural Bible

The Uniqueness of the Bible
- Written during a 1,500-year span
- Written over forty generations
- Written by more than forty authors from every walk of life
- Written in different places
- Written at different times
- Written during different moods
- Written on three continents
- Written in three languages
- Subject matter contains hundreds of controversial subjects
- Conclusion of continuity
—Josh McDowell, *Evidence that Demands a Verdict*, pp. 16–17

McDowell uses this list to correctly show that the Bible is a book that is unique above all others. His focus is on the concluding point, which states that, in spite of all the differences that could have occurred, the Bible has continuity in relation to controversial topics. He explains that a controversial topic is one over which people disagree. The Bible has impeccable continuity in all of the controversial topics it addresses. McDowell and others correctly believe this demonstrates that it had a single author. While this is important, I have come to a conclusion that does not include McDowell's final two points.

Most people would not consider the Bible to be a multicultural book. But when I look at this list, I see its multicultural aspects. People often say that the Bible is about only one people, the Jews, and their culture. While it is true that the Jewish people are often the focal point of the Bible, Jewish culture, like many others, underwent many changes during the writing of the books that comprise the Bible. As we will see, their ideas, customs, skills, arts, etc., along with their worldview and individual perspectives, changed greatly through the generations.

WRITTEN DURING A 1,500-YEAR SPAN

Moses began writing the first books of the Bible around 1440 BCE. The Apostle John wrote the final books sometime around 90 CE. This is a span of about 1,500 years. Over this amount of time any population's culture will change. Internal influences like technology, language development, economic emphasis, and population growth will lead to transformation, as will the exterior influences of trade, contact with foreigners, and immigration.

WRITTEN OVER FORTY GENERATIONS

Each generation has its own cultural variation; this is most readily apparent when several generations live together. Each generation has its own way of communicating, which is why parents, grandparents, and teenagers do not always understand each other. Values change within generations. What one generation believes to be important or necessary for survival or society is not necessarily valued by the next generation. Financial concerns may be the top priority with one generation, moral values may be the priority of the next, and ecological values the priority of the generation after that. Dress, music, and literature all change from generation to generation, even though each age group does seem to influence the ones that come after.

WRITTEN BY MORE THAN FORTY AUTHORS FROM EVERY WALK OF LIFE

Rich or poor, day laborer or corporate professional, workers all live in different cultures. The writers of the Bible represented various cultures based on the type of work they did.

Moses was a leader of Israelites when they left Egypt and moved around the wilderness for forty years. Prior to that, however, he was a well-educated member of Egypt's royal family, even though he was still a member of the oppressed Hebrew race. He probably suffered through racial slurs and was shunned, even as a member of the royal household.

Moses killed a man and then fled Egypt, becoming a shepherd in the wilderness.

Joshua was Moses's successor, spending much of his time in religious activity before becoming the military leader of Israel and helping to conquer the Promised Land. David was a shepherd who became a soldier and then king of Israel. Solomon, David's son, grew up in the royal court. Ezra and Nehemiah grew up in captivity in Babylon and Persia. Nehemiah—a cup bearer for the king of Persia, a very important and trusted position—helped rebuild the wall surrounding Jerusalem, which had been torn down when Babylon conquered the city. Jeremiah was a priest who was called by God to be a prophet when Judah was transitioning from being a free country to being conquered by Babylon. Daniel was a part of the nobility in Jerusalem, but he was taken into captivity by Babylon, where he became a trusted leader and served the kings of Babylon and Persia for many years. Amos was a fig-picking shepherd before he was called by God to be a prophet.

In the New Testament, Matthew was a tax collector for the Romans and was an outcast from Jewish society. John and Peter were fishermen from Galilee, an area despised by many Jews.[3] Luke was a Gentile, who was an associate of the Apostle Paul and believed to be a doctor. Paul was born in Tarsus, a city near the Mediterranean coast, but his family moved to Jerusalem so he could study under the best teacher of the day. A religious teacher and a Roman citizen, he was a member of the elite.

WRITTEN IN DIFFERENT PLACES, ON THREE CONTINENTS

The books of the Bible were composed in different places, each one connected more to an individual writer than to an overall culture. Therefore, each place speaks more to the context for the writer and the particular books he wrote. Yet it is important to acknowledge that place is a part of culture, and location likely affected the writer's view of the world. Moses wrote while wandering in the desert, and Joshua wrote in the land of Israel soon after the conquest. David was in a field herding sheep when he wrote some of the Psalms and in the palace as the king of Israel when he wrote the others. Most of the prophets wrote in Israel or Judah, but Ezekiel and Daniel were in Babylon during the captivity. Paul wrote from many cities as he visited different churches, and many of his works were written from jail cells.

One of the biggest indicators that the Bible is cross-cultural is that it was written on three continents: Africa, Asia, and Europe. These locales also had an influence on the text. Moses wrote in Africa as the Israelites wandered in the wilderness. At that time Egyptian culture was well known to the people. The land of Israel is part of the Middle East, which is on the Asian continent, and its customs and traditions are in line with Asian cultures. Those who wrote in Babylon or Persia, modern day Iraq and Iran, were also influenced by Asian cultures. The Apostle Paul wrote most of his letters as he traveled in Asia Minor, part of the area now known as Turkey. Paul also wrote from Rome, part of the European continent. Each of these areas has their own specific culture, each of which was taken into account by the writers.

Most of the Old Testament was meant for those living in the land of Israel, or those who were Jewish, while some of the first readers had not reached the Promised Land, and others were living in exile. Much of the New Testament was for the early church, which consisted of Jews and Gentiles in Israel, Egypt, Persia, Asia Minor, and Rome. These early churches were influenced by Greek philosophical thought and Roman legal theory. Since the Jewish synagogues were the first place the early Christians visited as they spread the message to each area, Jewish religious thought was also known in these churches. The first readers of Paul's writings were converts from Greek, Roman, or Eastern religions and were still surrounded by their temples and followers. These cultural issues were often addressed in the letters to churches and individuals found in the New Testament.

Written at Different Times

During the 1,500 years it took to write the Bible, Israel's culture changed many times. When Moses was drafting his first writings, Israel was populated by Bedouins who had just escaped from slavery in Egypt, one of the most technologically advanced societies of the time. The Israelites had been exposed to the technology, religion, and culture of Egypt, but now they had to establish their own.

By the time of Joshua, the people of Israel were learning how to be conquerors, taking over various cities, and then settling into an urban/agrarian society. The generation that had escaped from Egypt had passed away; a new generation was developing a new culture and also incorporated some of the religious traditions of the people they conquered.

Under the leadership of Saul, David, and Solomon, the people of Israel became a world power, which changed their culture and opened up more opportunities for connecting with outside influences. Israel was a hub for trade in the ancient world, which exposed it to a variety of cultures from

Africa and Asia. The Israelites learned about other religions, technologies, languages, and products from the merchants who passed through their borders on their way to trade with other countries.

By the time of the prophets, Israel and Judah were no longer a united power, and the people had to learn how to live as separate countries. The northern kingdom of Israel followed a pagan religion while the southern kingdom of Judah tentatively held on to Judaism. After many years, God exiled the northern kingdom to Assyria and the southern kingdom to Babylon. After seventy years, the Persians defeated the Babylonians and allowed the people of Israel to return to their land. Some, like Ezra and Nehemiah, returned, but many stayed in the other countries where they had built their lives.

Between the writing of the Old and New Testaments, Israel was dominated by Greece, and then by Rome, which had a powerful influence over thought, travel, trade, and religion. The people lived as an occupied nation; and these were the conditions when Jesus appeared on the scene. Paul wrote to Jews and others who were living under the influence of Greek and Roman thought, law, and tradition. The culture of Israel at the time the last books of the Old Testament and the New Testament books were written was very different from the culture during the time of Moses.

WRITTEN DURING DIFFERENT MOODS

A writer's mood is not really tied to his surroundings; however, it does speak to his worldview at the time and helps explain why he might have accepted or rejected certain parts of his culture. Looking at writers' moods also helps us to see the Bible as speaking to individuals and that the writing goes beyond cultural influence and touches the heart and emotions of writer and reader.

Not all the writers were ecstatically happy or even in a spiritual mood as they wrote. Jeremiah is known as the weeping prophet, and his prophecies against his people in Judah show signs of depression. He was depressed because of the people's wickedness and because he knew that they would soon be taken into captivity.

David was filled with joy and praise for God, and then fell into mourning and weeping and wondering if God had left him. He wrote psalms of praise as a shepherd and as a king, but when society rebelled against him, he cried out to God in grief.

WRITTEN IN THREE LANGUAGES

Perhaps the biggest indicator of the cross-cultural nature of the Bible is that the biblical writers used three languages: Hebrew, Aramaic, and Greek. Most of the Old Testament was written in Hebrew because Jewish people were its primary audience. However, a portion of Daniel is written in Aramaic, the language of the Assyrians and Babylonians who had conquered Israel. The book of Daniel was written for of the people of Israel who were in captivity in Babylon.

The New Testament is written in Greek, the language that had been used for trade since the time of Alexander the Great, similar to the way English is used today. Many people were bilingual; they spoke their native tongues but used Greek to trade and communicate with others. Using Greek as the language for the New Testament meant that many cultures could be reached simultaneously.

CONCERNING A CROSS-CULTURAL BIBLE

It's clear as one goes through this list that the Bible is a cross-cultural book. There must have been a reason for God to have used such variety within the writing. He could have waited until the second century and directed one person to write everything down in a single language. But its diverse nature suggests that the Bible is designed to reach all groups and time periods, and that God cares about all cultures, especially yours.

CHAPTER 2:
THE CROSS-CULTURAL
DESIGN OF THE BIBLE

HOW DO WE KNOW the Bible was designed to be cross-cultural? It is easy enough to pull phrases from the Bible and interpret them according to our culture, but this does a disservice to the Bible if it were not intended to be used in that way. Another way of phrasing this question is, how do we know that the Bible was designed to speak not only to the ancient Hebrews and first-century Greeks, but also to those who came after them as well? Let us look at the evidence that proves that the Bible was meant for more than the ancient cultures.

WORLDWIDE OUTLOOK
From the time its first books were written, the Bible has displayed a worldwide outlook. The early chapters of Genesis describe the origin of the universe and God's creation of the first humans. God did not create one place on the earth or one particular group of people. From Adam and Eve came all the people and the cultures they created. This is the list of nations referred to in Genesis 10, which chronicles the migration and expansion of the human population after Noah.

One of the core scriptures in the Hebrew Bible is Genesis 12 in which God promises to give Abraham land and heirs to inherit that land. God concludes his covenant with Abraham by promising, "In you all the families of the earth shall be blessed" (Genesis 12:3). Even at this early stage, God had a global outlook, which he conveyed to Abraham. From the beginning, it was clear that the Jewish people would affect the entire world. (Notice that the Bible does not say "some of the families"; it says "all of the families" will be blessed through the Jewish race, the descendents of Abraham.)

The next step for the Jewish people was to become the nation of Israel, which began to take shape during the time of the Exodus. God used Moses to lead the Israelites out of Egypt and into freedom. While they were in the wilderness, waiting to enter the Promised Land, they developed civil laws and established a governing body of religious leaders and civil judges. God established Passover (the Feast of Unleavened Bread) as an annual event to remind the people of how they had been delivered from slavery and bondage in Egypt. Interestingly, God also made a provision for those who were not Hebrew. Exodus 12:19 explains that if a stranger did not follow the rules of eating bread without yeast, he or she was to be isolated from the main group. Verse 48 states that those without Jewish blood can participate if they are circumcised. This shows that God was open to letting outsiders participate in Judaism and worship the Hebrew God. The worship of God was not to be limited to just one race or culture.

In Jewish tradition, there were two kinds of people in the world: Jews and everyone else (the Gentiles). Many Jews believed that God was Hebrew-centric, in other words, that God cared only about them. However, their prophets tried to change that mind-set. Isaiah wrote about the coming of a special servant of God who would bring justice to the Gentiles (42:1) and be a light to them (42:6). This servant was identified with the coming Christ, the future king of Israel, who would share God's message with the entire world, not just the Jews (49:6).

Luke described some events that showed the good news of Jesus was something for all people to hear, understand, and believe. Luke was a historian who traveled with Paul, which gave him opportunities to speak to and interview the other apostles, possibly even Mary, the mother of Jesus. In his Gospel, Luke relates the story of a man named Simeon, who saw the Holy Family in the temple as they were offering the appropriate sacrifice for the birth of Jesus. Simeon declared that Jesus was "a light to bring revelation to the Gentiles" (Luke 2:32). Jesus would be the one to open the door and allow the Jews and Gentiles to reunite with God.

Luke also wrote the book of Acts, and he relates the story of Paul and Barnabas in Antioch of Pisidia (Acts 13:44–48). Paul and Barnabas were speaking in the local synagogue. All was fine until a large group of Gentiles entered to hear what the two men were saying. This riled the Jewish leaders, and they began to argue with Paul, who pointed to Isaiah 49:6, the passage in which God says the Jews have been "given as a light to the Gentiles." The Jews were supposed to be the heralds of God's message to other nations, but they were failing this mission when they interacted with Paul and the Gentiles in Antioch of Pisidia.

Chapter 3 of the book of John describes a conversation between Jesus and a religious leader named Nicodemus. During that conversation, Jesus spoke some of the most famous words in the Bible. In John 3:16, he says, "For God so loved the world that He gave His only begotten Son, that whoever believes in Him should not perish but have everlasting life." God loves the entire world. The sacrifice of Jesus is for the entire world. Jesus did not say, "For God so loved Israel" or any other particular nation or group of people. This verse dramatically shows the global scope of God's love for humanity. The Bible, the Word of God, is the communication of love to everyone and therefore was made to be understood by all people and cultures.

Jesus does not only have a global outlook in that verse. In Matthew 28:18–20, the resurrected Jesus commands his followers to "make disciples of all the nations." The mission was not just to the Jews, it was to everyone. The disciples were to teach all the people what Jesus had taught them, which meant the message had be culturally relevant to all the different groups. Acts 1:8 solidifies this mission statement as the message was to be taken to "the end of the earth."

Revelation 14:6–7 describes an angel of God who has been given the Gospel to preach to everyone on earth. No one was to be excluded. Revelation 7:9–17 shows the result of this global vision. In this passage, people from every nation, tribe, and tongue are seen in heaven with God, having accepted the message of the Gospel. People from every culture understood the good news God had communicated and now lived with God for eternity.

As I look at the worldwide vision presented in the Bible, it strikes me that this book has to be from God. The Jews considered outsiders unclean and unworthy of God's love. Had they been the primary authors of the Bible, it would not have mentioned an outreach to the Gentiles. For example, the story of Jonah is exceptional, not because of the giant fish, but because Jonah did not want to give God's message to the Gentiles in Nineveh. In fact, Jonah was upset because God did not destroy the people of Nineveh (Jonah 4:1). Jonah is a prime example of what would have happened had the Bible been invented and written solely by humans.

Its premeditated global outlook shows that God was the author and was thinking about all cultures as he revealed the truth to the writers.

INSTANCES OF HISTORICAL AWARENESS

The Bible's writers often assume, as do almost all writers, that their audience is familiar with the customs and places they present in their narrative. But at times they either explain something to their readers or change a word to help a later generation.

For example, in the book of Ruth, the writer explains a strange custom related to the binding of a contract of which his readers may not have been aware: "Now this was the custom in former times in Israel concerning redeeming and exchanging, to confirm anything; one man took off his sandal and gave it to the other, and this was the confirmation in Israel" (Ruth 4:7). By the time Ruth was written, the culture had changed to such an extent, people were probably no longer familiar with the custom.

Likewise, in 1 Samuel 9:9, the writer defines the word *ra'ah* as "seers." The Old Testament almost always uses the Hebrew word *nabiy* to mean "prophets," a word that is also found in this verse. At the time, seer and prophet had the same meaning, and the writer felt compelled to point this out to his readers. Apparently, the writer's contemporaries would have understood *nabiy*, but not *ra'ah*.

Biblical writers sometimes used words that were familiar to their readers even if they did not fit what was being described. For instance, the word *heykal* usually means a large, structured building where people would meet or, more specifically, a king's palace. In 1 Samuel 1:9 and 3:3, it is used to refer to the temple in Jerusalem. However, what the writer is referring to is the *mishkan*, the tabernacle, a portable structure. The tabernacle was built during the time of Moses, when the Israelites were wandering in the wilderness for forty years. It served as a place of worship until Solomon built the temple. 1 Samuel must have been written at a time when people were familiar with the temple rather than the tabernacle. Both the language and the place of worship had changed, and the writer took note of these changes. The idea remained the same; both temple and tabernacle denote Israel's central place of worship. But by using the word *temple*, the writer helped the readers understand faster.

There is a curious verse in Genesis 14. It describes Abraham following the raiders who had captured his nephew, Lot. Verse 14 says that Abraham "went in pursuit as far as Dan." The problem is that the city of Dan did not have that name at that time. Judges 18:29 explains that the city's original name was Laish, and it was known by that name until long after Abraham. Around 1100 BCE, the name was changed by the Danites of Israel, who burned Laish and rebuilt it for their own use. This suggests that someone after Moses changed the name in Genesis so it would be culturally relevant to the readers of the day. It would be similar to an editor changing New Amsterdam to New York or Constantinople to Istanbul. Such changes help the current culture understand which places are being described in the narrative without diminishing its historical value.

Smith has examined this idea of cultural sensitivity within the Bible. One example he cites is that the words or concepts for salvation are different throughout the Bible depending on the culture being addressed: "The truth of salvation is not changed; only the expression in different cultural settings is changed."[4] The audience is the main focus of the Bible, not the people in the stories or the writers. Throughout the 1,500 years it took to write the Bible, there were many changes in the culture of the audience, "and with each change there [was] a change in the words, examples, and ways of telling truth."[5] When God communicates with humans, he is very sensitive to the fact that the culture in which they live affects their interpretation of what is being said. This is exemplified in the cultural sensitivity toward the first readers of the Bible.

Laws

Many laws are found in the Hebrew Scriptures, especially in the first five books written by Moses. These can basically be divided into two types: civil law and religious law.

Textual critics of the Bible have frequently said that the writings of Moses, who lived circa 1520–1400 BCE, were not original. They believe he stole the civil laws from earlier leaders like Hammurabi who ruled ancient Babylon from 1728 to 1686 BCE. Maybe some of the laws were similar, but I don't believe Moses broke any copyright laws. When it comes to declaring what is right and wrong and forming civil laws, God is the author of truth, no matter who writes it down. A good civil law is good for any culture; therefore, it cannot be copyrighted. For instance, it is wrong to steal another person's physical or intellectual property. That benefits society as it helps people to keep their possessions secure and encourages the development of new ideas. Could God have included civil laws that were familiar to other cultures to make the Hebrew Scriptures more culturally relevant to outsiders?

The first five books of the Bible also reference many religious laws, which deal with setting up the place of worship, observing sacrifices and religious festivals, priestly attire, and how priests should be purified in order to do their jobs, etc. Today, we can gain some insight into that world from the writings of Herodotus (490 BCE–circa 420 BCE), who was born in Asia Minor and traveled extensively throughout the ancient world. He wrote about the people and places he visited and about the Egyptian culture that would have been familiar to the first readers of the books of Moses.

For example, Herodotus tells us that the Egyptians practiced circumcision.[6] And the Bible says that Abraham visited Egypt before God said that circumcision would be the sign of the promise to Abraham's male heirs (Genesis 12:10–20 and 17:9–14).

Egyptian priests were all male, and each god had many priests, with one serving as high priest. When the high priest died his son took over the position.[7] This fits with Numbers 18:1–7, in which God sets up the line of succession and duties for the priesthood. Aaron was Israel's first high priest, and his sons succeeded to the position when he died. The priests in Egypt wore linen clothing, not anything made from animal skin.[8] A similar description is found in Exodus 28:31–39. The priests of Egypt were supported by the sacrifices and offerings of the people.[9] Numbers 18:8–32 addresses this law for Israel.

Animals had to pass a test before they could be sacrificed.[10] Throughout the Old Testament, such as in Leviticus 1:3, there are references to sacrifices having to be perfect. The animals had to be blemish free before they could be considered an appropriate sacrifice for God.

All of these ideas from Egypt were instituted by God, through the commands he gave for proper worship and running the temple in the books of Moses. While God did institute some new rituals, he also incorporated some of the familiar Egyptian customs into the new Hebrew religion and gave them new meaning.

Jesus boiled all of the religious and civil laws into two simple ones: love the Lord your God with all your heart, soul, mind, and strength, and love your neighbor as yourself (Deuteronomy 6:4–5, Mark 12:29–31, Leviticus 19:18, Matthew 22:40). The first was the religious law; the second was the civil law. All laws, whether made by humans or God, must follow these two rules in order to be good.

DEPICTIONS OF THE MESSIAH

The preeminent focal point of the Bible is the Messiah (Hebrew) or the Christ (Greek). The interesting thing is that this person is seen in various ways by different writers. Their descriptions are similar enough to make it clear that the same person is being described, but each writer has his own cultural lenses and is writing in a way that is relevant to his society and readers.

One of the more prominent names for this person is the Servant.[11] The first readers of the Bible would have been familiar with servants as they were a part of their lives. As Willis Judson Beecher writes, the author of chapters 40–66 of Isaiah, "being a Hebrew-speaking person, follows the Hebrew idiom when he applies a personal name to a nation."[12] In other words, when he wrote about the Servant, the writer was using an idiom that was culturally accepted by the Israelites. Many of the mentions of the Servant in Isaiah are references to the nation of Israel, but there are times where the term refers to an individual on a mission to Israel.[13] The writers of the New Testament pointed to the Old Testament passages regarding the Servant and showed how they appropriately referred to Jesus.[14] In other words, the writers of the New Testament did not ignore the culturally accepted idiom that equated the Messiah with the Servant. They embraced it.

Messiah was another term that was popular with the prophets during the Divided Kingdom.[15] *Messiah* is transliterated from the Hebrew, and our English word *Christ* is from the Greek translation of the Hebrew word. It simply means "anointed one," and in historical writings it was used to indicate an appointed king or sometimes a priest or prophet. Some of the prophets used the term to refer to a future king, a descendant of David, who would rule the kingdom of Israel.

After the captivity in Egypt, Israel was controlled by Persia, then Greece, and finally Rome. During the Greek occupation, the people of Israel began equating the Messiah with a king who would come, lead Israel to freedom, and set up a new, independent kingdom. By the time of Jesus, Israel was under the rule of Rome. The Jews hated the Romans and wanted to live in a free nation as they had under King David. They focused on the passages of the Hebrew Scriptures that described the coming of a king, like David, in the hope that this person would overthrow the Romans and allow them to have their own nation and government again. The Messiah was a symbol of freedom and power for many generations of Jews.

Hhasidh, another term found in the Hebrew Scriptures,[16] is translated as holy one, merciful one, godly one, gracious one, and in the plural as saints.[17] This word is only found in poetry and refers to God's favor being on or flowing through someone. The people believed that particular favor would be shown to the Messiah.

God's Son is another term used to identify the Messiah, although it generally refers to the king of Israel, a descendant of David. This term becomes prominent after its use in 2 Samuel 7:14 when God promises David, "I will be his father, and he will be my son." From that point on, the rightful kings of Israel are referred to as sons of God. This passage does not describe Jesus, though, because the next sentence contains the phrase "if he commits iniquity." In the New Testament, Jesus is called "the only begotten Son of God" (John 3:16). This means that Jesus is the true heir of David for whom Israel had been waiting. Jesus is the only real Son of God and the king of Israel.

David calls this future king "Lord" in Psalm 110:1. David was the high king of Israel. All the kings who came after him would follow his authority. However, this particular king would be greater than David. Jesus posed the question to the religious leaders, "If David called him Lord, how could this person be David's son?" (Luke 19:41–45). The people of Jesus' time were looking for a human king, but Jesus used the words of the Hebrew Scriptures to show that this person would be not only David's heir, but the heir of God, who is higher than David.

The New Testament writers frequently used "Lord" to refer to Jesus. The Greek term, *kurios*, reflected the Hebrew word for God—Adonai.[18] The New Testament writers expected that their readers would understand the importance of the word based on their knowledge of the Hebrew Scriptures. Many of the first Christian converts to Christianity were Jewish or had converted to Judaism and would have been familiar with the scriptures.

Other terms are used in both the Hebrew Scriptures and the New Testament: Elect or Chosen One, Branch or Flower, Regent, High Priest, Last Adam, Word, Wisdom, and Redeemer to name a few. The point is that God was not satisfied with using just one term to describe this coming Savior. God wanted people to see the Messiah in ways that were culturally and personally significant to them. Thus, he gave us not only a broader picture of the significance of Jesus's ministry but also the ability to see him within our own cultural lenses.

Therefore, it is perfectly acceptable for someone from Latin America to identify with the crucified Christ; for a poor person to identify with the poor Jesus who walked the earth; for a person with disabilities to identify with the Jesus's "imperfect body," which had holes in it after the resurrection.[19] Some believers see Jesus as representing wisdom. Justo Gonzalez relates to Jesus as the carpenter who was oppressed by the ruling class.[20] Virgilio Elizondo identifies with the Jesus from Galilee, a rejected part of Israel that was constantly looked down on for its non-Jewish cities and its poor economic situation.[21] Some African cultures consider Jesus to be the chief, the ancestor, or the healer.[22] Each culture identifies with Jesus in ways that are legitimate to Jesus's ministry and his relationship to the group. The many terms within the Bible gives us the freedom to see Jesus in many ways and in a way that is relevant to us personally.

MULTIPLE AUTHORS AND GENRES

As we've studied the composition of the Bible, we've found that various writers and genres were used to communicate God's message. The question is, did God do this intentionally? The answer is yes. By using more than a single individual from a single culture or one type of literary method, God ensured that many different people would understand the Bible.

This can be equated to a shotgun-like effect. God has used many different projectiles to hit the target, which is to have his message understood by all cultures and individuals. As Smith says, "when message and message styles are matched between producers and receivers, the intended meaning is more likely to be formed by the audience."[23] In other words, I have a better chance that you will understand my message if I match my presentation style to a style you are familiar with and can accept. Surely each of us can identify with a writer or character within the Bible, or latch onto a type of literature that we can understand.

Jeannine Brown points out that "Genre choice has much to do with the determination of how an author communicates, for different genres communicate in distinct ways."[24] In other words, an author makes a statement simply by choosing a certain genre to present his message. If the writer wants to stir emotion, poetry might be the best choice in some situations. At other times, a logical argument in the form of a letter might be more successful. Narratives and stories excite the imagination as our minds fill in pictures of characters and scenes. The activation of the imagination also helps the reader or listener to absorb the message of the story.

Middle Eastern societies are known for people who express themselves with poetic words full of metaphor and simile. This type of speech anchors the message within the deep emotions of the person,[25] and is characteristic of the poetry in the Bible. Many Westerners, however, seem more comfortable with the letters within the Bible, especially those written by Paul, because they are so straightforward and linear.[26] Biblical narratives are suited to cultures in Africa, Asia, and South America, or any place where stories are told and the listener has to find the meaning on his own. The narratives of the Bible are an indirect form of communication and give the meaning or moral indirectly.[27] Poetry, letters, and narratives are but three of the genres within the Bible. Even with just these three types, God would be able to communicate with most of the cultures of the world. God chooses the proper genre for conveying his desired message.

The Bible's writers all had various social and economic backgrounds in addition to the wide time spans between them. "Inspired by the Holy Spirit," writes Smith, "the message was nevertheless shaped by the containers into which it was poured."[28] Daniel, Ezra, Nehemiah, and Ezekiel lived in a land that was not native to them. Moses understood the horrors of slavery and prejudice. David knew what it was like to be both a manual laborer worker and the head of a country, and how his relationship with God was affected by these circumstances. Jeremiah suffered from depression and anxiety. Matthew knew what it was like to be despised by his own people. Jesus, John, and Peter understood what it was like to be demeaned and ridiculed because of their economic status and their birthplace. Paul had first-hand knowledge of the consequences that result when one changes from belief that is popular to one that is persecuted. "These communicators expressed the truth they perceived in the images and experiences of their lives," notes Smith.[29] God had each of the writers use their experiences to shape the message he wanted to send to everyone on Earth.

ON THE DESIGN OF THE BIBLE

Based on the few examples given in this chapter, it is clear that God designed the Bible to be cross-cultural. The Bible clearly has had a global outlook from the very beginning and has not been tied to one particular race or culture. The variety of authors, language, and genres shows God's desire to communicate and reach all the cultures of the world.

CHAPTER 3: THE BENEFITS OF TRANSLATION

ONE OF THE QUESTIONS related to finding meaning through communication is, what language is being used? Proper communication cannot happen if a person cannot understand what is being said. There has to be some form of comprehension, even if that means using an interpreter.

THE DIASPORA

There was a time when the people of Israel were driven from their land and placed in other countries because they did not follow God. This scattering began in 586 BCE when the Northern Kingdom of Israel fell to the Assyrian Empire. Assyria displaced the Jews and put them into the area northeast of the Mediterranean, the area we call Asia Minor. This dispersion of the people is called the Diaspora.

In 722 BCE, the Southern Kingdom, Judah, fell to the Babylonian Empire, which also took over the Assyrian Empire. This extended the Diaspora all the way to the Persian Gulf, the area now held by Iraq and Iran. Some of the Jews at this time also fled to Egypt where they set up strong communities.

Then Babylon was conquered by the Persian Empire, which spread Jewish communities as far east as the Indus River in Pakistan and India, and as far north as the Aral Sea in what is now Russia. The Persian Empire was defeated in turn by Alexander the Great of Greece. Much of the Greek Empire then fell to Rome. However, some of the Persian Empire rose from the ashes—specifically, the land between the Persian Gulf and the

Indus River—and lasted beyond the time of Jesus. The Greek and Roman conquests opened up the European continent to Jewish communities.

Jewish people could not help but adapt to the cultures in which they were living; however, they also kept much of their own culture. Many of those who were exposed to Greek philosophy and culture adopted that culture, leaving behind some of their Jewish heritage. In many of the countries, Jewish people did not have a temple as a central place of worship. They built synagogues in each community, where they prayed, read the scriptures, sang hymns and observed the Sabbath. The synagogues provided the early bases of operation for Christian churches in the different regions of the world.

THE EARLY CHURCH

Even though Jewish people under Persian rule were allowed to return to the land of Israel, many chose to stay in the countries where they were making lives for themselves. Very few returned to the homeland. For example, there was a significant Jewish community within the Persian province of Babylonia. Between 200 and 600, the Babylonian Talmud, a systemized commentary of Jewish law, was written and compiled near Baghdad.[30]

Jewish communities were widespread, as evidenced by the comments of the first-century historian Josephus. Speaking about the wealth in the temple at Jerusalem, Josephus commented, "let no one wonder that there was so much wealth in our temple, since all the Jews throughout the habitable earth, and those that worshipped God, nay even those of Asia and Europe, sent their contributions to it, and this from ancient times."[31] Josephus also describes the extent of the dispersion during the first century.

According to Josephus, the dispersed Jews were well thought of in the empire: "The Jews also obtained honors from the kings of Asia, when they became their auxiliaries; for Seleucus Nicator made them citizens of those cities which he built in Asia, and in the Lower Syria, and in the metropolis itself, Antioch."[32] This put the Jewish population in a great position; those who later became Christians and began to spread the Gospel held great credibility and influence with their neighbors and leaders.

During Pentecost, there were representatives from the dispersed Jewish communities in Persia, Iraq, Turkey and Asia Minor, Egypt and other parts of Africa, and Rome (Acts 2:8–11). Three thousand of them were converted on the day of Pentecost (Acts 2:41). They then went back to their own communities and established churches and Christian communities. The very first verse of the Epistle of James is directed to the Jewish communities of the Diaspora. In the first verse of chapter 2, James appears to be speaking to Jewish Christians.

The early church included writers and teachers from various parts of the Roman and Persian empires. Clement (30–100) was a Roman Gentile who was at Philippi in Macedonia (ancient Greece) with Paul. Polycarp (65–155) was bishop of Smyrna in Asia Minor. Ignatius of Antioch (30–107) wrote to Rome, Ephesus, Magnesia, Tralles, and Philadelphia (Alaşehir) and Tarsus, both in Asia Minor. Papias (70–155) was bishop of the church in Hieropolis, Phrygia. Irenaeus (120–202) of Lyons sent missionaries into other areas of Gaul. Tatian (110–172) was from Assyria, and Theophilus of Antioch (115–181) became bishop of Antioch in 168. Antioch (in Syria) was one of the most influential of the early churches, exceeding to some extent the Church of Jerusalem. It was the church at Antioch that commissioned Paul and Barnabas's mission to the Gentiles (Acts 13:1–3). Antioch became a center for Christian teaching and had great influence on doctrine.

A city that had equal, if not more, influence on teaching than Antioch did was Alexandria, Egypt. Clement (153–217) was a teacher at the School of Alexandria. Origen (185–254) was Clement's pupil and succeeded Clement as head of the school. This school greatly influenced the leaders of the church. Gregory Thaumaturgus (205–265) was born in Neocaesarea, the main city in Pontus, and studied under Origen in Caesarea in Judea. Dionysius (200–265) also studied under Origen, ran the school, and became bishop of Alexandria in 246. Julius Africanus (200–245) was a student of Heracles, Origen's successor, and was the bishop of Emmaus in Israel.

Alexandria was not the only church in Africa to produce scholars. Cyprian (200–258) was the bishop of Carthage from 248 to 258 and an influential teacher. Minucius Felix, who had held the position of advocate at Rome, was a product of the Alexandrian and Carthaginian schools after his conversion to Christianity.

So far we have not mentioned Rome. "Even at the close of the Second Century," writes A. Cleveland Coxe, "the Church in Rome is an inconsiderable, though prominent, member of the great confederation of Christian Churches which has its chief seats in Alexandria and Antioch, and of which the entire Literature is Greek."[33] In the European mind, Rome always seems to be prominent, but the church there was more a product of the schools of Antioch and Alexandria. Hippolytus (170–236);

Caius (180–217), a presbyter of Rome, and Novation (210–280) also a presbyter of Rome, helped strengthen the Roman church's leadership and scholarship.

The early church spread out from Israel into Syria, Asia Minor, Greece, Rome, and Africa. There were congregations in Persia as well since many Jews settled there and never returned to the land of Israel. Other reasons made this area rich for Christianity. First, it was on the trade routes that connected the West to the East. Second, "because of its location—close to the Roman frontier, but just far enough beyond it to avoid heavy-handed interference—Mesopotamia or Iraq retained a powerful Christian culture at least through the thirteenth century."[34]

But the church did spread beyond the reach of the Jewish faith as it made its way to India. According to tradition, the Apostle Thomas went to India and preached the Gospel and planted the church there. Egyptian Christian records show that there was a continuing Christian presence in India during the second century. John of Persia and India attended the Council of Nicea in 325.[35]

When the shah of Persia was deposed in 497, he ran to the Huns for protection, taking with him some missionary companions. Five missionaries stayed for seven years while two laymen remained for thirty years. During this time they took the oral language of the Huns and created a written language, teaching them to read and write.[36] They also helped with agriculture. These actions helped spread Christ's message to the Huns and into eastern Asia toward China. In 635, "Persian missionaries reached the capital of the T'ang-dynasty in China and before long were converting the migrating Turkish tribes of central Asia."[37] The first Christian church was built in the Chinese capital of Chang'an in 638, which at that point was the largest city in the world.[38]

Without the Diaspora forcing the Jews into various countries, where they formed synagogues, the church would not have had a strong transcultural base in which to operate. It easily could have been confined to Israel or its surrounding countries. The two major theological schools at Antioch and Alexandria accounted for the scholarship of the Christian leadership, not just in theology, but in philosophy, rhetoric, apologetics, and literature. This growth allowed the leaders to be people who were sought out for their knowledge and allowed them to interact with various cultures when they presented the Gospel message.

TRANSLATIONS

Since the ancient church was so widespread over Europe, Africa, and Asia, there was a need to translate the Bible into the vernacular language of the local communities. As Justo Gonzalez points out, not only did this give access to people who did not have access to the Bible before, it also became "the people's book, no longer under the control of those who control society."[39] The Bible was not to be relegated to a few people who could read an ancient or foreign language and who, therefore, would have all of the power within the church. Remember, the Bible is a pillar of the church, and whoever controls the biblical interpretation controls doctrine. This was born out when Pope "Benedict insisted that authentic Christianity *had* to be based on the Greek philosophical tradition, establishing the European intellectual model as the inevitable norm for all future ages."[40] This meant that whoever wanted to interpret the Bible and remain in line with the Catholic Church had to use that method of interpretation, which used European culture as the standard. All other cultures had to adhere or be deemed heretical. It is the epitome of arrogance to believe that one culture holds the key to the interpretation of the Bible. This is why it is important for the Bible to be translated into multiple languages.

One of the first translations was of the Old Testament. Around 320 BCE, Alexander the Great conquered Egypt and founded the city of Alexandria. By 285 BCE, Alexander was dead, and his empire had been divided among his generals. Egypt was ruled by Ptolemy and his descendants. Ptolemy Philadelphus, the king of Egypt was interested in literature and had a large library that he filled with the latest writings. He maintained contact with many of the Jews living in Alexandria and was aware of their scriptures. He commissioned seventy men to translate the Hebrew Scriptures into Greek so they could be placed in his library. Once this was completed, the Greek translation, called the Septuagint, became available to the Jews in Alexandria. As the Jews grew more distant from their Hebrew culture and more Greek in their culture and speech, this copy of the scriptures became useful to them.[41] We know that this translation was prominent during the time of Jesus and the apostles because many quotations from the New Testament reflect the Septuagint rather than the Hebrew Bible.

This Septuagint was written in everyday Greek, the same language used in the New Testament, which was the language used for trade in the world at that time. This allowed the Bible to be relevant to many cultures in the world, especially in the eastern Mediterranean where Greek was the prevailing language.[42] To use a different language or an academic language that was not understood by the masses would have been detrimental to the spread of the Gospel. Charles Craft states, "Such language, though appropriate in other times and other places, hijacks a message that might otherwise have been perceived as relevant and induces a perception of irrelevance."[43]

The Peshitta was a Syriac translation of the Old and New Testaments produced in the 100s. Syriac was the language of the Asian church[44] and helped take the message to people in Asia Minor and Persia. Around 170, Tatian the Assyrian translated the four Gospels from Greek into Syriac. He combined the four books into a harmony of the Gospels called the *Diatessaron*, which placed the texts side by side according to subject matter. A measure of the importance of Bible translation in the growth of the church can be seen in that it was not until Tatian completed his *Diatessaron* that Christianity spread into the Asian countryside, where Syriac was the common language.[45] Sometime before 431 the New Testament portion of the Peshitta received an upgrade through the efforts of Rabbula, bishop of Edessa. He translated it from the Greek into Syriac, and separated the Gospels into four books, like the original Greek version, instead of using Tatian's combined *Diatessaron*. Philoxenus, bishop of Mabbogh, translated the entire New Testament, including the book of Revelation, into Syriac in 508.[46] Syriac "became the ecclesiastical language of the Church of the East as Latin became the language of the Western church."[47] Without these translations the church of the East would have remained closed to the common people and the expansion of Christianity into those areas would have been greatly reduced.

In the early 400s, Jerome translated the Bible into Latin. This translation is called the Vulgate and was the standard for the Catholic church for centuries. It helped Christian culture and thought in Western Europe develop in Latin.[48]

By the sixth century, Persian missionaries were penetrating deep within the heart of Asia and finding it necessary to translate the scriptures into the languages of the people there. Some even managed to translate parts into the language of the Huns.[49]

During the eighth century, a leader named Adam rose in the church in China. He was "a bishop and missionary-scholar so famed for his knowledge of Chinese language and literature that even Buddhist missionaries came to him for help in translating their sacred books."[50] Adam was not from the church of Rome, but the church of Persia. He translated portions of the Bible, such as the Gospels and Paul's Epistles into Chinese to help his missionary endeavor in that culture.

Other translations came during the Middle Ages. The Biblia Alfonsina was a Spanish translation by King Alfonso the Wise of Castile in the late 1200s. In the late 1300s, John Wycliffe produced one of the first English translations. Martin Luther translated the Bible into German during the Reformation in the early 1500s. Luther wanted the people, and not just the priests who knew Latin, to have access to the Word of God; at that time, the Vulgate was the only sanctioned translation of the Bible. In 1590, there was a translation into Hungarian called the Karoly Bible. Perhaps one of the best-known translations is the 1611 King James Version.

The translators all had one thing in common: they wanted to give the Bible to the people. "The Bible was originally in the language of the common people," writes Charles H. Kraft, "language that required no academic degrees, no knowledge of history to understand."[51] Literacy was a factor, as it still is in some areas of the world today. The common custom was for someone to read the scriptures to the congregants. This was true in the synagogue and in the early church. It was not until the printing press was invented around 1440 that literacy rates began to increase due to the availability of written literature. Before that time, most cultures dispensed information orally.

The Bible was originally written in Greek and Hebrew, which were easily understood by its first readers and listeners. However, as those languages became less popular, and as the Gospel spread into areas where those languages were not known, it became necessary to translate the Bible by using the most accessible language possible. The translators of the King James Version asked, "But how shall men meditate in that which they cannot understand? How shall they understand that which is kept close in an unknown tongue?"[52] Each translator saw the difficulty people had with the versions that were available to them and chose to take the Bible back to where God intended it to be. God used very little technical language in the original; he used down-to-earth language that people could grasp easily.[53] The work of Bible translation continues today with the same goal of making it accessible to people so they don't need a degree in ancient languages or history to understand it.

A FAILURE TO COMMUNICATE

Using translations is a great tool for reaching people with the Gospel, but what are some possible consequences of failing to do so? Let us look at what happened in the Arabian Peninsula. For more than three hundred years, Christians lived in the peninsula, but by the time of the Prophet Mohammed (570–632), no translation of the Bible in Arabic could be found. Originally, Mohammed was open to the message of the Old and New Testaments, but without an Arabic Bible, he had no access to the true message and had to rely on fragments that did not adequately represent the truth. Some contend that if the Bible had been translated into Arabic, the religious history of that region would have been significantly changed.[54] In other words, people will reject the message if it is not in a form that they can understand and study for themselves. Kraft notes that "if biblical content is presented in such a way that the receptors do not perceive it to be relevant, the verdict concerning communication is that the Bible is not relevant to them."[55] It is much harder for people to see relevance in something that is not communicated in their own language. They give up trying to understand it. This becomes a barrier to the Gospel message.

Another consequence of not taking the time and effort to translate the scriptures into the vernacular is postulated by Moffett. He states that it gave the impression that the Christians in Persia and Byzantine Syria were culturally insensitive or racially prejudiced against Arabs.[56] He notes that missionaries from the same Asian churches had already translated the Bible into Syriac, Chinese, and less familiar Asian tribal languages, but had made no attempt to translate the scriptures into Arabic. This action, or rather, inaction, gives the impression of prejudice, whether or not it was present. Today, there are still some languages without a Bible translation. These are small groups of people, mostly with an oral culture. But are we giving that same impression of prejudice by forcing people to learn a language that is not their own so they can understand the Bible?

If a main pillar of the church creates a stumbling stone for people, then we are doing a disservice to the Gospel. Since language is constantly changing, accurate, updated translations of the scriptures in the vernacular of a culture are crucial to the message of Christ and the health of the church.

SECTION II:
COMMUNICATION

Chapter 4: The Basics of Communication

Communication can be described as one person trying to express his thoughts to another. The communicator expresses his thoughts, while the receiver or receptor attempts to make sense of what has been stated. That is a simple way to put it, and one that everyone can understand. However, there is much more to communication than this simple definition can account for.

Every day you communicate with others without having to think through the process. It seems natural. But from the moment you are born you have been taught how to interact with others. Certain rules must be followed for there to be communication between two people. In this chapter, we will ask a series of questions that will help to form the basis for the rules of communication. At the end of the chapter, we will take a closer look at those rules.

You communicate with other people in many ways: in person or on the phone; by using gestures and body language, sometimes unintentionally; using words, characters, and symbols to text, e-mail, blog, tweet, or write a note, letter, or report. Sometimes you use pictures, such as emoticons or photographs.

When I teach people how we communicate, I put the following phrase on the board: "I will never forget today." I then ask the question, "What do we need to know to figure out what is being communicated in this sentence?" The class usually is able to come up with most of the items that are needed to understand what is being communicated. Most people do know how communication works and perform it without thinking about it. It is not rocket science or something that is beyond your ability. It is a function of life that you use every day, and you already understand how it works. Interestingly, the questions we must answer are the same no matter what the culture of the communicator. That is why they can form the basis for the rules of communication. We are looking at communication among human beings, not a particular culture. So let us look at some of the questions that must be answered.

WHICH LANGUAGE IS USED?

In the beginning all humans spoke the same language. It was not until after the flood that the various languages were created. The people began to build a city so they could stay together, which violated the command God gave to Adam, Eve, and Noah's family to populate the whole earth (Genesis 1:28, 9:7). God then created other languages. The people soon grouped together according to language and moved away from each other, fulfilling God's vision of humans populating the earth.

The world is full of different languages, but most people have a native tongue that is used in the places where they grew up. Each group has its own way of speaking as there are particular words or phrases, colloquialisms and idioms, that are understood by those within the group, but may not be understood by those outside. There is a difference in the idioms used by a person from a rural community and those of a person from an urban area.

Immigrants face the challenge of learning the language of their new country. Those who are bilingual have to decide what language they will use to communicate with another person. It would be disruptive for the immigrant to use his native tongue to talk with a native. But the immigrant could easily communicate with his own family using his native tongue.

Each job or industry has its own jargon. Computer people definitely have their own jargon, as do mechanics, bankers, insurance people, and religious people. Even short-order cooks have a lingo all their own. Each workplace has its own shorthand for communicating. A new person to the job has to learn the shorthand to communicate, and a person outside of that line of work might have no idea what was being said. Groups of friends will also create their own languages to communicate with each other.

Every time you communicate you must decide what language you are going to use. Will you use your native tongue, or will you use the language of those around you? Will you use the shorthand of your friends or coworkers, or the more conventional language of people who are not in those groups?

When we look at the phrase "I will never forget today," we need to know if it was written in a language that we can understand. Is it my native tongue? Then maybe the message was meant for me. Is it some form of shorthand used by my friends, coworkers, or some other group? If it is from one of them, the meaning will be a little different than if it were a more formal correspondence. Knowing which language has been chosen will help us understand something about the communicator and the person(s) for whom the message was intended.

WHAT GENRE IS USED?

The written word is usually divided into genres or types. If you go into a bookstore, you will see sections for romance novels, history, science fiction, cookbooks, and biographies, among others. All of these are genres, and bookstores tend to be arranged so that we can easily find what we want within a particular genre. There are other kinds of writing, including personal and business letters, a note to a friend, a set of instructions, a legal code, a poem, a diary entry, or a school paper. With so many types available, which genre you decide to use is important when you communicate with others. Each genre will convey a different meaning to the other person.

"I will never forget today." Was that found in a story, a school history report, an e-mail to a friend, or a poem? Knowing what genre the phrase fits into helps identify what the author intended to convey. The phrase is not a genre in and of itself; it must be couched in a genre to have real meaning. This is called context.

WHAT IS THE CONTEXT?

Context actually has two levels. First, context is considered the words and paragraphs around a certain part of writing. In other words, to get a clue about what "I will never forget today" means, we should look at the rest of the document in which it is found. What was the author writing about when that phrase was used? What did the author write about after the phrase was used?

This type of context helps us understand a person's train of thought as he uses certain words or phrases. It is what is usually meant when you hear someone say that something was taken out of context. In this sound-bite world we live in, it is easy for people to take just a fraction of what someone has said and then distort it into something that was not intended. We see this happen with political campaigns as one party tries to take one sentence out of an opponent's thirty-minute speech and show how wrong he is on a particular issue. Sometimes friends will only hear part of what you say and will get the wrong impression, causing tension in the friendship.

Second, the context is the situation a person is in at the time of the communication. The next few questions will help us break down this type of context. It involves knowing the history of the person, his values and culture, as well as where and when he is writing. It is usually referred to as the cultural context.

What Is the History of the Communicator?

Knowing a person's history helps clarify his communication. Is he an immigrant, or did he grow up in this country? Were his parents first-generation immigrants who had to learn a second language, one for their family and one for those outside their family? Did he live in poverty or wealth? Was he raised on a farm or in the inner city? What kind of education did he have? A person's multiple experiences make up his history and influence how he communicates.

A person's ancient history is not the only thing that creates a cultural context of communication. Near and current events also create the context. When we look at the phrase, "I will never forget today," it is probably the current cultural context that will provide the biggest clue. Was the person who wrote it suffering a trauma, such as the death of a loved one, or a joy, such as a proposal of marriage or the birth of a child? Knowing the circumstances that surrounded the author as he was writing the phrase will help identify its meaning.

What Are the Communicator's Values?

Values, those things each person holds as socially acceptable and important, influence how a message is sent and received. What a person thinks about family, money, country, or friends can help determine his values. Does the communicator assume that the receptor will have certain values, or is the communicator communicating from a certain set of values? Someone who considers family to be important will tend to understand communication that centers on family. He also will assume that others hold family to be important and will use that value in his communication with others.

Knowing how someone defines his values is also important. In some cultures family is considered everyone in a community, not just the nuclear family of parents and siblings. In this type of culture to fail at a task is to dishonor the community. This must be understood in order to properly understand what that person is communicating. Both people could value family, but if their definitions of family are different, it could cause confusion.

If someone were to value family strongly, he might write, "I will never forget today" when his parents divorce, at the death of a grandparent, or at the birth of a child. Someone who highly values business or money might write the same phrase after the loss of a big contract or an extreme drop in the stock market.

What Is the Communicator's Culture?

Culture can be defined in many different ways. Basically speaking, culture is the shared social values and lifestyle of a group of people. It can include economic standing, religion, art, literature, and other forms of communication. Each person's culture heavily influences how he communicates.

What Is the Communicator's Physical Context?

Location does affect communication. If we are among friends, we will be more open with our use of language and in the way we express ourselves. The opposite is true if we are with our boss or meeting with an important business client. In those situations we tend to use more formal language and express ourselves in a more formal way. But even with these people there can be exceptions due to where we are. We will be more open with the boss during a dinner party than we would be at the office. The place where something is communicated is a part of the context. For instance, knowing that the person who wrote "I will never forget today" was writing from the Eiffel Tower in Paris will have a different meaning than knowing he was writing from a hospital in the United States. Knowing the place also helps us understand the culture and language surrounding the person at the time of the communication.

When Was the Communication Given?

Knowing when someone communicates a message is also an important part of the context. A communication from the Pilgrims in North America in the 1600s would have a different context than a communication during the Revolutionary War. And both would have different contexts than a communication from someone living in the United States today.

THINGS THAT CONFUSE MEANING

In addition to helping us identify the meaning of some communication, the previous questions can also help us see which things cause communication to break down. When the answer to a question is unfamiliar, it makes it hard for us to fully understand what the other person is trying to say.

Sometimes there is a language barrier between the communicator and the receptor. Neither person understands the language of the other. Interpreters can help in this area, but interpretation is not an exact science. Inflexion and colloquialisms can be lost in translation.

Genre actually helps to stabilize meaning, because it helps communicate both the message and its tone. However, if the receptor does not understand the genre, the message can get confused. To read a fairy tale as if it were historical literature would confuse the story. To read poetry as prose would lead to a misreading of the figurative language and a misunderstanding of the poem's message.

Context also helps to stabilize the meaning, but if the receptor does not understand the context, confusion is the result. We find this a lot with the Bible. People either fail to understand the writer's historical and cultural context or they disregard the written context surrounding a phrase or passage. When we do not understand the context, we tend to replace it with our own, which leads to confusion and misunderstanding.

If we do not understand someone's history, we may not fully understand what they are trying to communicate. Sometimes we have to trace the long history of a people, not just the short history of the speaker or author. For instance, we might not understand why a wealthy person in a respected position might say he is oppressed by his boss. We might think he is just joking. However, if this person comes from a group or family that has been oppressed for generations, it will leave a scar on him and influence his communication.

Failing to understand the values someone holds can cause a barrier in communication. When we do not share the same values as someone else it becomes a sticking point. One person might approach a subject based on family values, while the other person considers social values to be more important. The two people may be attempting to solve the same problem, but they cannot succeed because they misunderstand the values that are driving their communication.

Language and genre choices are wrapped up in culture. And culture has had influence on a person's history and values. If we cannot understand the culture of the person attempting to communicate with us, we will have a very difficult time trying to understand. This is probably where the main disconnect occurs when people try to understand the Bible, and it really should not be this way. Some believe that if they cannot understand the Bible's culture, they will never be able to understand how the Bible could possibly apply to them. But we do not need to have a full understanding of another person's culture to get some meaning from the conversation. The more we know, the better we will understand, but we will never know everything about a person. The same is true of the Bible. We can pick up the Bible without knowing anything about its culture and still be able to garner some meaning. It is true that the more you know, the more you will gain, but it is not true that we must know everything to get something out of it.

If we think someone is in a different place or time than he really is when the communication originates, we might have a skewed understanding of what is being communicated. To read Shakespeare while disregarding his origins in Elizabethan England would produce another barrier to communication. Many have updated Shakespeare's plays to modern times and cultures. Still, each person had to begin with the playwright's original context in order to understand his writing and transpose it to another place and time.

WHAT ABOUT THE RULES?

As I see them, the rules for communication, and there is much debate in this area, are relatively simple. First, we must ask the right questions. That is what we were trying to accomplish in the first part of this chapter. Second, we must have the right answers to those questions. Third, we must adhere to the correct answers when we are trying to obtain meaning. These seem to be basic to any culture.

Let me demonstrate. If I look at a portion of the Bible, I must first ask questions about the genre and the author. Let us say that it is a psalm of David. As I read the text, I will ask questions about the textual and historical/cultural contexts. David may have penned this psalm in response to some trouble he was having with others, and the part I am reading is his cry to God for help. From those questions, I generate answers. If I have a correct answer, then I am in a better position to understand the meaning. An incorrect answer may inhibit my ability to understand the passage. Once I have the correct answers, I cannot discount them and come up with my own meaning. That will place a barrier between the communicator and the receptor. In other words, I cannot say that the passage is a prophecy if it refers to something that happened in the past.

A good example can be found in Exodus 14 and 15. These two chapters describe the same event—the crossing of the Red Sea by Israel and the destruction of the Egyptian army. Chapter 14 is a historical text written in prose, a narrative account of what happened, full of facts and description. Chapter 15, however, is not prose. It is a song, full of poetic words and forms. To ignore the genres of these chapters creates an incorrect interpretation. If we say chapter 14 is poetic, then we can discount the miraculous crossing of the Red Sea. If we set aside the fact that chapter 15 is a song, then we can find errors in its description of the crossing. It is important that we stay true to the answers to our questions.

- Ask the right questions.
- Obtain the right answers.
- Do not dismiss the correct answers and substitute your own.

These are the basic rules for communication, and the rules we should follow when interpreting the Bible. Breaking the rules will lead to misunderstanding.

CHAPTER 5:
THE STEW OF MEANING

MANY SMART PEOPLE HAVE tried to explain how we get meaning out of the symbols and sounds we use to communicate. In the previous chapter, we examined some of the questions whose answers either aid or hurt our understanding about what is being communicated. My theory is that meaning is like a stew. The communicator puts in his ingredients, and the receptor puts in his ingredients. The problem is that the ingredients, the answers to the questions we asked in chapter 4, are not always the same. "This means," notes Kraft, "that when you get right down to fine details, no two people ever attach exactly the same set of meanings to any given symbol, no matter how tight the group they are in."[57] No two pots of stew are going to be exactly the same.

You might be thinking, "Can't we just go to the dictionary to find the meaning?" This is a legitimate question. According to the compilers of Webster's Dictionary, "The dictionary is primarily a record of how the words of a language are used by those who speak and write it as a mother tongue."[58] The compilers of a dictionary do not make up words and give them meanings. They listen to people speak, read what is written, and then place the meanings used in those contexts in the dictionary. The compilers of Webster's continue: "Dictionaries do not tell their users how they *ought* to speak and write the English language, but only how they *can* do so and what other speakers and writers think about the options available to everyone."[59] Language is constantly evolving and changing, to the point that the dictionary can only give meanings that people can use. Not only are new words created, but old words receive new meanings. The word *gay* used to mean happy, bright, and buoyant. Now it is a synonym for homosexual.[60] The old meaning is no longer the most prevalent. As noted in Webster's, "No dictionary can include all meanings of its words, because those meanings are ever expanding."[61] It is the context of the word that gives us the meaning of the word at any particular time.

Each person brings his own perspective to what is being communicated. Whether he is the communicator or the receptor, he will look at the communication from his point of view, and evaluate it according to his language, history, values, and culture. Each person assumes that the other party understands how he is evaluating the communication. Failure to see the other person's perspective is why we sometimes have a hard time understanding each other.

While it may hamper understanding at times, seeing things from different perspectives is good. Very rarely is there only one way to look at something. When you look at a section of the Bible from your own perspective, it makes that section meaningful to you. The ability to see the same text from another perspective broadens your view—of another person or culture, the Bible, and the God who wrote it.

Even when we have a hard time seeing the other person's perspective it does not make it impossible to understand what is being communicated. As Smith says,

> Nevertheless, we can develop meanings that are approximately the same between two individuals. To do so requires careful learning of (1) the original context and (2) the receiver's context, and it also requires (3) concentration on transferring sufficient information.[62]

We may not be able to get a one-to-one agreement, but the more we understand about the communicator and the receptor, the closer to the meaning we will get.

Think about when you first meet someone. You may not understand his jokes or the way he says some things, but you can still communicate. The more you get to know that person and learn the answers to some of the questions, the more you are able to understand him and why he says things the way he does. Another person who has just met your friend might think he is weird, but you know him well enough to know that he is not; he has his reasons for expressing himself the way he does. You understand your friend's stew of meaning. "People living in different cultures, however, have fewer similar or shared experiences than do those living in the same culture," writes Smith. "Therefore the development of similar meaning becomes more difficult."[63] When we look at the Bible we are confronted by our culture and the Bible's culture. This makes it more difficult, but not impossible, to understand the meaning. A problem arises when people attempt to match the ingredients in their stew to those in the biblical writer's stew without knowing which cookbook was used. We do not have to know the answers to all the questions, but knowing at least some of them helps us to understand what the writer wanted to convey.

Some people have a hard time connecting the Bible's culture to their own. However, the stories within the Bible go deeper than just superficial cultural variances. Biblical narratives display the root culture of humanity, the way we think and act as humans. Therefore, the Bible is relatable to all cultures because every culture has a human component. People are not that different from each other. Since the Bible is a cross-cultural book and can speak to anyone, there always will be some point of common contact. In other words, the stew of the Bible will relate to our stew in some meaningful way.

Genre plays a large part in the stew of meaning. "When message and message styles are matched between producers and receivers," writes Smith, "the intended meaning is more likely to be formed by the audience."[64] In other words, if the person trying to communicate can use a genre that the receptor can understand, then there is a better chance the communication will be understood. For instance, if I referred to a science-fiction movie, my point would be lost if you had never seen the movie or did not like the genre. However, if you were a science-fiction fan, then my point would connect with you in a meaningful and memorable way. By the same token if someone loves to read poetry, a good way to get a message across to them might be to put it in poetic form. If a person likes reading books about history, communicating through the historical genre would help to connect with him. Surely everyone can find some genre in the Bible that appeals to him as there are poetry, songs, action, adventure, narrative, history, and letters, among others. The different genres take into account people's various communication styles and learning methods, allowing God to reach everyone with the truth.

Our stew of meaning includes another set of ingredients: our predispositions. "Individuals have *predispositions* to listen to particular messages and reject others," notes Smith. "Based on their anticipation of satisfaction from particular messages, individuals *self-select* what they will pay attention to."[65] We hear what we want to hear. People who see this phenomenon in their spouses call it selective hearing. We tend to listen more attentively if the topic is something we like or if it will benefit us. We will listen to someone who tells us how great we are, but tune out the boss who constantly berates us for no reason. We have a predisposition to dislike listening to rules, even if they are for our benefit. If you doubt this, ask some airline attendants how many people pay attention to their preflight talk about security exits and flotation devices. In the same way, people pay attention to the parts of the Bible that they like or that benefit them. They can read about God's love all day long, but can't sit still for a minute when the Ten Commandments are presented.

This idea of predispositions can be seen in 2 Samuel 11–12, which relates the story of David and Bathsheba, the adultery and killing of the latter's husband Uriah, and the subsequent condemnation of David by the prophet Nathan. The interpretation of Nathan's story that I'd always heard from the pulpit focused on the adultery and murder. No mention was made of the abuse of power. Those who are in positions of power, whether they are leaders, rich, or the majority population, have a predisposition to interpret this story in a certain way. In my classes, I conduct an experiment that begins with a reading of Nathan's story (2 Samuel 12:1–6); then the students report on what they believe the story means. Without fail, these people determine that the story is about the abuse of power, rather than adultery or murder.

Prior knowledge is also an ingredient in our stew. At times, we develop blind spots because of something we have learned previously. We then interpret any further information based on prior knowledge, even if it was wrong. For instance, as I was writing this book, I gave some people rough drafts of certain chapters and asked them for feedback. Brother Bernard, a national pastor in the Democratic Republic of Congo, pointed out that I'd mentioned the "angel of death" when I described the Passover story. He gently said that his Bible did not contain those words and that it appeared that God was the one who passed over, not an angel. Somewhere along the way I had been taught that an angel of God passed over Egypt, much like the story in 2 Chronicles in which David saw an angel wiping out Israel. Every time I read Exodus 12, I unconsciously placed an angel into the story. When I reread the passage carefully, I discovered that Brother Bernard was right. God, not an angel, passed over Egypt, which makes the story entirely different and stronger. We must always keep in mind that our predispositions and earlier experiences and learning can hinder our ability to understand and communicate with others.

Here is one more example that focuses on three parables, the Lost Sheep (Luke 15:3–7), the Lost Coin (Luke 15:8–10), and the Lost Son (Luke 15:11–32). We get a variety of interpretations from well respected scholars. Justo Gonzales, who was born in Cuba and emigrated to the United States, says, "The three parables are not originally addressed to the lost, but to those who feel left out because Jesus is eating with the lost: to those who have never been lost."[66] He sees Jesus speaking to the ninety-nine sheep instead of to the one. The sheep are to reach out to the margins of society. According to Stephanie Buckhanon Crowder, the parables reflect God reaching out and finding those who are lost or in a spiritual wilderness.[67] Because many people in his culture are walkers, Paul John Isaak sees the parables as an analogy to our walking with Jesus as he searches for the lost.[68] None of these interpretations is wrong. But they do show how our experiences can influence our interpretations of the scriptures.

The Ingredients for the Stew of Meaning

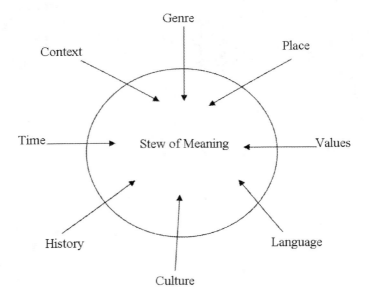

CHAPTER 6:
HOW GOD COMMUNICATES
WITH HUMANS

WE JUST DISCUSSED HOW we communicate with each other. We also listed some of the questions we need to answer before we can find meaning in what is being communicated. Now let us turn to how God communicates with people.

REVEAL
To reveal means to present that which was hidden. Revelation is the method by which knowledge about God is transferred from God to people or from person to person. The purpose of revelation is to teach people about God, themselves, and the relationship between God and humans. One of God's chosen methods of revelation is communication, which God gave humans the capacity to understand and use.

Revelation must come from the one who is being revealed. Therefore, revelation is not the same as knowing. Revelation is only a part of knowing. We cannot know God unless he reveals information to us. Knowing is a human action, but revealing is an action undertaken specifically by God. We can learn about an animal by observing it in its habitat or by dissecting it. We can find out about a suspect by interrogating him. But we cannot get to know God in that way. The action of revelation must be undertaken voluntarily by God. We cannot find God in order to study his person and personality.

The very act of revealing brings forth characteristics of the revealer. The revealer must have some cognizance of himself and of others. The revealer must be a being rather than an object. The revealer must have some purpose in revealing. The very act of revelation is intimate and personal. Such an act contradicts those who say God is aloof and uninvolved in human affairs.

Revelation is not a static or single action; it is a continuous process that is different for each person, time, and culture. Since the purpose of God's revelation is to teach people about him, each individual must be exposed to the revelation in a personally relevant way. Thus, God uses the learning styles and the communication methods of the contemporary culture to reveal truth to each individual.

THREE FORMS OF REVELATION

God desires to have a relationship with all of creation, especially humans. Communication is a basic part of any relationship. Therefore, God wants to communicate with people. God is the source of truth and wants to reveal truth to us—about himself, about ourselves, and about our relationship with him. God has chosen three ways to reveal truth: generally, specifically, and relationally.

General revelation has been universally recognized by scholars and is defined as God speaking through creation. The Apostle Paul pointed this out in Romans 1:20, when he wrote that God's characteristics have been clearly seen since the creation of the world. The writer of Psalm 148 also understood that people praise God by declaring the truth about him. Just as people use works of art to communicate something about themselves or others, God uses nature to communicate the truth about his creativity, power, and intelligence. As we study the earth and the universe around us, we learn things that God wants us to know—things that are true. We see the vastness and organization of the universe and understand that God is vast and larger than anything on the earth. We also learn that God is a careful planner, who puts things in order instead of allowing them to remain chaotic. A simple rock can amaze us with its strength, and we know that God is stronger than the rock. A trip to the zoo helps us see God's creativity in giving us so many different animals. In these examples, God is saying, "I am larger than you can imagine, stronger than anything you've seen, and more creative than you realize."

General revelation is impersonal. There seems to be no real live communication between us and God. It is like looking at a piece of art when the artist has long since died. We can guess what the artist was getting at, but we cannot ask him any questions. General revelation is an indirect way of divulging truth.

The second form of revelation is specific, which is when God speaks to people directly. The greatest—and according to some scholars, the only—example of specific revelation is the Bible. God spoke to individuals and told them to write down certain truths about his relationship with human beings (2 Timothy 3:16). While specific revelation is direct, it is limited because it is in a set format, the written word, and from a specific time. After all, there are no modern updates to the scriptures. However, the Bible is written in such a way that it is able to speak truth to any person in any culture and in any period. The writers of the Bible and the first readers were not the only ones who could gain the truth revealed by God. As Smith says, "The written message has many advantages. It is not bound by constraints of time, distance, or personal contact. It does not change with each reading, so it can remain authoritative as a check on the correctness of what is spoken."[69] Specific revelation may be limited in the amount of information revealed, but it is not limited as to audience or time.

Relational revelation refers to Jesus's communications with individuals during his ministry or the Holy Spirit living within Christians and guiding them in the truth. The Holy Spirit's job is to reveal truth directly to people (John 15:26, 16:7–15, 8:16). This is different from specific revelation, which is more general in nature and directed to the masses. Generally speaking, the truth revealed through relational revelation is targeted at an individual or a small group. Obviously, the words of Jesus can fit into both categories, but the interaction between the Holy Spirit and the individual Christian fits into relational revelation more than any other category. Relational revelation is very personal and direct. It is God speaking directly to an individual in a personally meaningful way. Relational revelation is also unlimited because the Holy Spirit is available to all and there is no set form of communication.

All three forms of revelation can be seen in Hebrews 1:1–2. The author began his letter in verse 1 by describing God talking to the writers of the Hebrew Bible, which is specific revelation. In the first part of verse 2, the author explained how God spoke through Jesus, which is both specific and relational revelation. Finally, at the end of verse 2, the author mentioned that Jesus was a part of the act of creating the universe, which is a reference to general revelation.

General and specific revelation are for the masses and deal with interpretation. Thus, we focus on what they mean, which truth is being revealed. With relational revelation, we focus on how to apply the truth to our individual lives.

ALL THREE MUST AGREE

These three forms of revelation form a protective border around the truth God communicates to people. If one side fails, then the truth will be exposed to error; it will be tainted, and humans will not know the real truth. All three must agree. The reason this is important is that throughout church history, various people have chosen to place more importance on one part of revelation over the others. This has always led to a misunderstanding of the truth. It is similar to not having the right answer to one of the questions we ask to determine meaning. Unless all three of these revelations agree, we cannot understand what God means to communicate.

Jesus did not present anything new. He only pointed to what was there. The Holy Spirit does not present anything new, only what is there. When we misunderstand, it is not the revelation but the interpretation that is flawed. When the interpreter does not use his tools properly or relies on his own thinking and wisdom, the interpretation will be wrong, but the revelation still will be true. My concern is that too many people think God stopped speaking in 90 CE, and that he has nothing to say to them today. All revelation comes from the same source. There is a single revelation communicated in different ways. We should not forget that the Holy Spirit is still teaching us as we study the revelation of God. We are not stuck in the four hundred silent years between the Old and New Testaments. The Holy Spirit is still active within and around us today, teaching truth to those who want to know it.

THE LANGUAGE OF REVELATION

God could have used a language and a culture that would be revealed only to a specific few. But he used human language and customs to convey his message to all people, and continues to do so today. Kraft calls this "receptor oriented" communication.[70] The receptor is the focus, and the communicator tailors his method of communicating in a way the receptor will understand. Kraft says that God "has had to do all the adjusting, allowing us to be the ones on familiar ground. It is an indication of his love, acceptance, and respect for us and a mark of his receptor-orientation that he has chosen our frame of reference rather than demanding that we use his."[71]

Types of Revelation

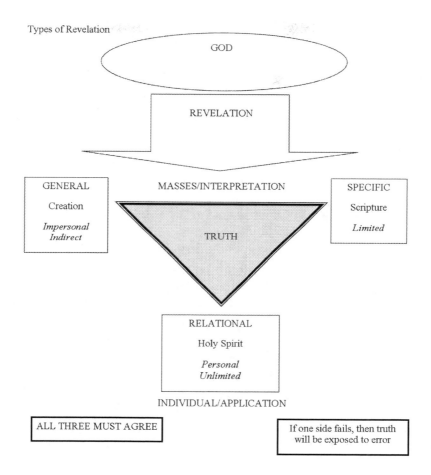

The Father, Son, and Holy Spirit communicated with each other long before humans were created. It is doubtful that the language God used is one that can be found on Earth today or at any time in human history. Had God decided to use this language, there would be no way for humans to understand or comprehend the truth he was attempting to teach them. However, God is wise. Instead of teaching people another foreign language, God used the language of the people who were involved in the development of the Bible—the writers, readers, and listeners. God "employs *our* language and culture to get his ideas across to us, agreeing to the meanings that we attached to those symbols."[72]

Part of the book of Daniel is written in Aramaic. This is a significant example of God's cultural sensitivity as well as his use of a literary style to make a point. Daniel was a Jewish person writing during the time of captivity and was among the first to be deported to Babylon. Prior to the captivity, Israel had traded with other countries where Aramaic would have been the language of choice. Thus, the Israelites in captivity would have been familiar with both Hebrew and Aramaic.

The book begins in Hebrew (1:1–2:4a) and describes the move from Israel, where Hebrew was the native tongue, to Babylon, where Aramaic was spoken. The transition from Hebrew in 2:4a to Aramaic in 2:4b seems to correspond to the transition from freedom to captivity. It is in this passage that the author focuses on the Babylonian king's court and life in captivity.

Daniel continues in Aramaic and relates life within captivity up to chapter 8. While the book presents other visions concerning various nations, chapter 8, verse 1 includes the first vision of "the Glorious Land," i.e., Israel. In this vision, Daniel talks about sacrifices that will be made in a rebuilt temple in Israel, a reference to the people returning to and rebuilding their homeland. The captivity would not last forever. The author of Daniel seems to highlight this by transitioning back to Hebrew, the language of Israel. The prophecies after this one, as well as a prayer, all relate to the Israelites living once again in their own land.

Through the transition from Hebrew to Aramaic and back again, God, through Daniel, was telling readers that their captivity will not last. They will speak Hebrew in their own land again. God will not abandon his promise to Israel. God's use of two commonly used languages shows his cultural sensitivity and his desire to make his message clear.

For the New Testament, God chose the Greek language. It would have been easy to choose Hebrew again, since many of the early church members were Jewish. God also could have used Aramaic, which was popular in Israel, but it was falling into disuse in the rest of the Roman Empire. Since the New Testament was written during the height of Roman dominance, God could have chosen Latin. However, Greek was the most prevalent language in the world at that time; it was used for trading, much as Aramaic had been previously. While not everyone spoke or understood Greek, the vast majority did understand it, particularly in the areas where the New Testament was written. God, in his wisdom and practicality, used the most popular language to reach the greatest number of people possible at the time.

Furthermore, God did not use the high Greek that was reserved for plays and poetry. Instead, he used the Greek that was spoken or written during business transactions and personal correspondence. To use an illustration from English, the difference between the two styles of Greek is like the difference between a play by Shakespeare and your local newspaper. God used the style to which most people could relate.[73]

As Francis Schaeffer writes,

> The personal God has made us to speak to each other in language. So, if a personal God has made us to be language communicators—and that is obviously what man is—why then should it be surprising to think of Him speaking to Paul in Hebrew on the Damascus road? Why should it be surprising, in communicating to man in a verbalized propositional, factual way that He should tell us the true truth in all areas concerning which he communicates?[74]

In other words, it should not surprise us that God communicates to us in a language that we understand. God invented language and communication so there would be relationships between humans and between God and humans. It seems obvious that God would use the form of communication that would reach the intended audience. The use of Hebrew by the early writers of the Bible shows that God's audience at that time was mainly Jewish people, who were to be his representatives to the world. The later use of the Greek language shows that God had a more transcultural, international audience in mind for the message in the New Testament.

God also speaks on topics that are important to humans. Kraft says that God "deals with topics of pressing relevance to his hearers, topics that usually relate to needs that are both real to his interactants and perceived to be important by them."[75] It would have been easy for God to talk about things that are important in the heavenly realm but not on Earth. However, that approach would not have communicated anything to humans. God chose to convey the truth about real human needs. In this, way the Bible's message transcends cultures by relating things that are true to all humans, not just those of a certain group.

USE OF LAWS AND RITUALS

There are also examples of God using human laws, customs, and rituals to communicate with people. We have already looked at some of the religious rituals from Egypt that God allowed the Jews to use in their worship. God uses narrative to relate the truths. Kraft describes the Bible as "a collection of case histories, recording specific personal encounters within specific socio-cultural contexts."[76] The stories are about real people in real situations within real cultures. God gives us a picture that all can identify with by showing people as they really are, in their natural habitat, so to speak.

We find reference to customs and narrative teaching in Genesis 15, where Abraham questions how God will honor his promise about the heirs and land. Starting in verse 9, God commands Abraham to bring animals for sacrifice. Abraham obeys and splits the sacrifices in two, placing half on one side of a path and half on the other. Experts disagree about whether this was a known custom for closing a deal. Some commentators believe that two parties entering into a contract would pass between the sacrifices, each one swearing by their God to uphold the contract. Others say that this custom cannot be found anywhere other than in Genesis 15. If we look at the passage in Genesis closely, we see that God does not instruct Abraham about what to do. Abraham simply does it. In addition, no explanation is given to the reader about what is going on with this ceremony. These two points suggest that this was a known ritual that was familiar to the first readers of the Bible. In other words, God used a manmade ritual to inform Abraham that he would uphold their covenant. God was the only One who passed between the sacrifices (Genesis 15:17–18). This was a covenant made by God to Abraham, not a contract between God and Abraham. (A covenant is upheld by one person; a contract must be upheld by both parties.) This would have been very clear to the first readers of the Bible, who knew the meaning of the ritual.

The fact that this was a known ritual is also supported by a passage in Jeremiah 34. Beginning in verse 8, we find that the people of Jerusalem have entered into a covenant giving the slaves their freedom. This covenant is then broken, and the slaves are returned to slavery. God rebukes the people of Jerusalem for breaking the covenant and promises that the consequence will be death and destruction. The interesting passage is verse 18, in which God mentions the covenant and people walking between a calf that has been cut in two. The people ratified their covenant with the slaves by walking between two altars, each containing half of a sacrificed calf. This signified that they swore by God to uphold the covenant, and that God would punish them if they did not do so. Apparently the custom Abraham followed in Genesis was still prevalent at the time of the divided kingdom, which explains why Moses did not feel the need to explain the passage in Genesis. This was a human custom that God used to explain a greater truth. God even retained the meaning humans had given to the ceremony by punishing those who failed to uphold the covenant.

The Code of Hammurabi (laws 196–200) includes an eye-for-an-eye penalty after injuring someone. The same punishment can be found in Leviticus 24:19–20, and Leviticus 18:6–18 lists laws against sexual relations with relatives that are similar to laws 154–58 in the Code of Hammurabi. A stele from the 23rd century BCE confirms Herodotus's report that circumcision was a religious ritual in Egypt.[77] God gave this ritual greater significance when it was tied to his promise to Abraham in Genesis 17.

Knowing the communicator's values is important. The Bible promotes God's values, not human values. The Great Communicator teaches us true values that are the heart of God and how these values affect our relationships with other people.

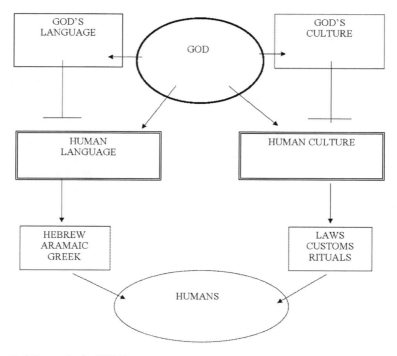

God Communicating With Humans

THE HOLY SPIRIT'S WORK

The central influence, or conduit, that God uses to communicate with people is the Holy Spirit. The Holy Spirit inspired the Bible's original writers to write the truth God wanted to convey. This was done in such a way that the writer's cultural identity was not lost. God was able to use cultural peculiarities such as language, history, genre, and context to make the truth accessible to the writer and his readers.

The writers of the Bible were no different than any other writers in that they kept their audience in mind. The writer's stew of meaning influenced his work, but he had to be aware of the receptor's stew of meaning to adequately communicate the truth. The Holy Spirit helped this process by illuminating the first receptors as they read or heard the text. The first receptors had to take into account the writer's stew of meaning as they tried to understand the truth being conveyed. This was part of the illumination process enacted by the Holy Spirit. Another part of the illumination process was to help the first receptors apply the truth to their daily lives.

The Holy Spirit's work did not stop with the writers and the first receptors. The Holy Spirit illuminates all who want to understand the written truth. Today, we have to try to understand the writers' and the first receptor's ingredients and then figure out how they apply to our ingredients within our stew of meaning. The Holy Spirit helps us with this process and helps us apply the truth to our particular situations. This is why the Bible can speak to any individual in any culture. This is the relational revelation part of the communication process between God and humans.

God uses common human communication skills to deliver the truth through the Bible. Any method of interpretation must have these skills at its core to be viable. The method must also take into account the current receptor's stew of meaning as God does when he communicates through the Bible.

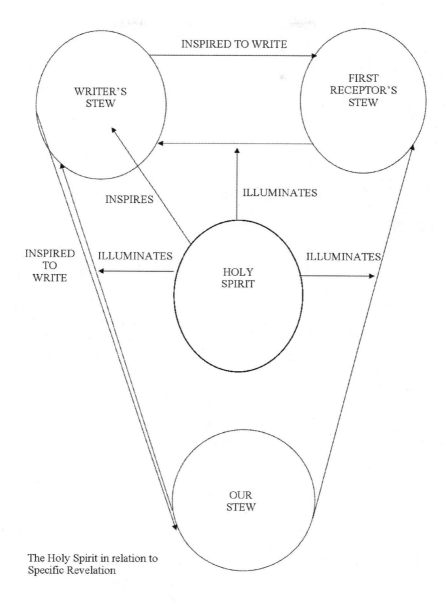

INSPIRED TO WRITE

WRITER'S
STEW

FIRST
RECEPTOR'S
STEW

ILLUMINATES

INSPIRES

INSPIRED
TO
WRITE

ILLUMINATES

HOLY
SPIRIT

ILLUMINATES

OUR
STEW

The Holy Spirit in relation to
Specific Revelation

CHAPTER 7: THE BASICS OF HERMENEUTICS

HERMENEUTICS IS A WORD that is thrown around in Christian intellectual circles. While the method of hermeneutics is a matter of great debate, the definition is fairly simple: "the art or science of the interpretation of literature."[78] We apply hermeneutics when we study the literature of the Bible; the method we use is called a hermeneutic.

There are many different types of hermeneutics. Hermeneutics are usually tied to the culture of their designers. James Cone uses an African American–centered hermeneutic; Justo Gonzalez uses a Hispanic-centered hermeneutic. Some hermeneutics are centered on the culture of ancient Israel. Most hermeneutics available today, however, are Eurocentric. Cain Hope Felder notes,

> There is, of course, much biblical study that goes on in North America and other regions besides Europe, but the conventions, the standards, the procedures, and the assumptions of biblical scholarship, like those of nearly every field, have been set and fixed by white, male, European academics over the past several centuries.[79]

We cannot ignore that Europe and the United States have been at the center of hermeneutical studies for the past few centuries, or ignore that these studies are male dominated.

All of these hermeneutics are valid and have some value to the cultures in which they originate, which is evidence that the Bible truly is cross-cultural. However, it is difficult for those using a culturally specific hermeneutic to help others gain meaning from the Bible because a person has to learn about the particular culture before the hermeneutic can be used.

Since the Bible is cross-cultural, it allows for various hermeneutics, but it also permits a transcultural one. God wants to speak to all people and has given us a text that does just that. Why wouldn't there be a hermeneutic that is transcultural? If God communicates through a cross-cultural book there must be a transcultural way to understand that communication.

We have already discussed the fact that God wants to communicate to the masses. The scriptures are written in the common language of the people, although God could have used an unknown language that would be revealed only to a select few. In the sixteenth century, the leaders of the Reformation saw that the church at that time practiced an elitist view in which only the priests could access and interpret the scriptures. Ordinary people were not allowed to study the Bible on their own. The Reformation, in part, was sparked by a desire to wrest the scriptures away from the dominance of the elite clergy and bring them back to the people as God had intended.[80]

Today, we seem to be headed in the same direction as the church was heading prior to the Reformation. We have made the interpretation of the Bible an exercise that only academics and intellectuals can conduct. While we give lip service to the fact that anyone can interpret the Bible for themselves, the truth is that we look to the pastors and teachers who have graduated from the seminary to lead the way in interpretation. There is value in education and in having various methods of interpretation, but God also wants to communicate directly through the scriptures to the masses, not all of whom have such an education.

There is an assumption within many hermeneutics that the biblical author's precise meaning can be found. When this assumption is placed with a culturally centered hermeneutic, it can cause a problem. William Meyers puts it this way: "It is preoccupied with the notion that a text has only one legitimate meaning, which usually means *the* only orthodox meaning."[81] This assumption is usually identified with the Eurocentric model of hermeneutics; it implies that this model is the only way to interpret the text without cultural bias, and that all other methods of interpretation must be judged by it and are inherently culturally biased.[82] It gives the impression that the only orthodox or precise meaning is inherently Eurocentric and binds the Bible to European culture. Any culturally centered hermeneutic will suffer the same limitation. The one who controls the hermeneutic controls the "orthodox" meaning.

The chapter on communication briefly touched on the fact that there cannot be a one-to-one correlation in meaning between the communicator and the receptor.[83] The rules for communication do not demand a one-to-one correlation in meaning. This means that we cannot always communicate exactly what we mean. Sometimes our ability to communicate hinders us; at other times, it is the receptor's ability to understand. Our stews of meaning get in the way of our communication. This chapter is a good illustration of this point. I know what I want to say and what I mean, but the words and methods of communication bar me from being able to express those thoughts completely. Undoubtedly, readers will ask questions and for clarification about what I have written. However, people can still grasp what I am attempting to communicate because I do not expect them to understand my precise meaning.

Since we cannot reach a one-to-one correlation for meaning between the communicator and the receptor, we allow for shades of meanings that are close enough for the two parties to agree that communication has been achieved. I call this shaded area of meaning the "allowable meaning," and it is not without its boundaries. The communicator helps to set the boundaries of the meaning, so we can still accurately say that someone did not understand what we meant, that he was wrong in his interpretation. However, the allowable meaning is broader than the precise meaning.

No matter what process we devise for interpretation we will always be unable to obtain the precise meaning. Therefore, those hermeneutics that assume we can locate the author's precise meaning will always fail as it is an impossible task. Their advantage is that they seem to be able to get close to the precise meaning; however, they are still only within the allowable meaning.

Surely God, who created communication, would also allow for variance. This would mean that there are parameters for meaning within the Bible. There are interpretations that are wrong and miss the meaning altogether, but the meaning is not as confined as previously believed or taught. As a cross-cultural book, the Bible must allow for a variety of interpretations on the part of the receptor.

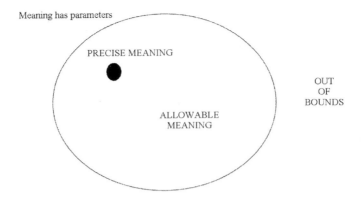

By saying that there is an allowable meaning in the scriptures, we automatically think about the boundaries of that meaning. All viable hermeneutics must observe the proper rules of communication. They must ask the right questions, get the correct answers, and then not replace those answers with their own. If those rules are violated, then no communication can occur, and we will not be able to get real meaning from the scriptures. Therefore, the rules of communication form a boundary that cannot be crossed.

We have already discussed another set of parameters: general, specific, and relational revelation. Those three must agree with any interpretation or meaning that we think we get from a text. It is important to note that, since God is the author of the entire Bible, the scriptures are the best interpreter as God would not insert contradictions the way that multiple human authors could. This helps set the boundaries within the text itself. But another component will help us determine the boundaries of meaning: looking at the past communities of Christians and the meanings they found; the modern communities of Christians and the meanings they find; and the modern individual who is conducting personal study and finding meaning for his life. Unlike the three types of revelation, the three communities will not always agree. Yet they still help us to see boundaries, as they can define what is out of bounds for all and what is in bounds for any particular culture. The communities must make sure that they are within the bounds of the rules of communication, and that none of the three types of revelation disagree with their interpretation, for it to be within the bounds of the allowable meaning.

Look back at the theologians of the Middle East, Europe, or any other area of the world and see how they interpreted various passages of the Bible. Church synods helped to define some interpretations in relation to doctrine and are useful in finding the allowable meaning as well as defining what is out of bounds. We can review the discussions about the church in all cultures to see what decisions have been made about which interpretations appropriately followed the rules of communication and therefore fit into the allowable meaning. These discussions also may point out where people have failed to adhere to the rules of communication and in so doing stepped out of bounds in interpretation.

By using the three communities to define the boundaries, we will find it helpful to understand some of the stew of meaning of the communities and the interpreters. God, through the Holy Spirit, communicates meaning to people within their own cultural settings, just as he communicated to the Bible's original writers and receptors. We can see how truly cross-cultural God's communication with humans is by expanding our vision beyond the receptors of biblical times. Looking at the interpretations of past Christian communities helps us to stop limiting the Bible to the ancient past; looking at modern interpretations encourages us to see that God is still communicating to us through the Bible. The great thing about this part of the process is that we are not confined to a single community; therefore our hermeneutic does not become centered on any particular culture.

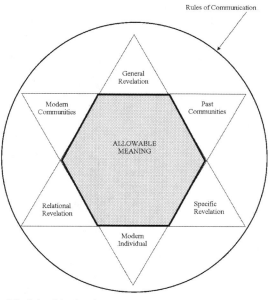

Setting the boundaries of meaning

Now that the false assumption of a precise meaning has been set aside and the boundaries for allowable meaning have been set, we have a better picture of how modern people from all around the world can find meaning in the Bible. God has given a broad enough allowable meaning for the scriptures that can be interpreted and related to by each culture. Sometimes the meaning is the same for multiple cultures, but at other times one culture will take away a meaning that is specifically relevant to it. This allows various hermeneutics to be valid, as long as they remain in the allowable meaning and do not transgress into the out-of-bounds area. The allowable meaning is broad enough to handle the needs of various people.

Another assumption that hinders most of the current hermeneutics is that only by knowing the original human writer's stew of meaning can we properly interpret the scriptures. It suggests that only by knowing the original historical context of the writer and the first receptors can we truly grasp the intended meaning. William Meyers notes that this type of hermeneutic "reads the text solely as a product of history. Thus, in its search for original meaning it effectively locks the text in the past."[84] This creates a hermeneutic that is centered on the culture of the original writer. While knowing the writer's stew of meaning is beneficial, focusing merely on those data hinders us from observing the meaning for current cultures.

The Bible was written by humans, but it was not authored by humans. On this point, every Christian should be able to agree. The Apostle Paul told Timothy, "All Scripture is given by inspiration of God" (2 Tim. 3:16). The true author is God. However, when we look at many of the models for hermeneutics they look a little like this:

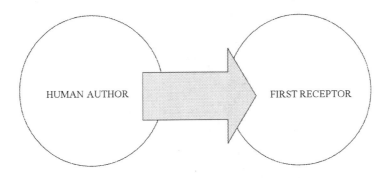

Common Hermeneutical View of Authorship

This model states that by knowing the original author's intent regarding the original receptors we can find the meaning of the communication. There are two profound problems with this theory. First, much of the Bible developed through oral traditions or compiled records, and we do not know the true original authors. Second, the human writers were not the original authors. God is the original author; therefore the model should look more like this:

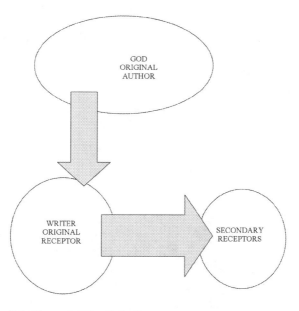

Biblical Hermeneutical View of Authorship

The writer of the book of Hebrews says, "God, who at various times and in various ways spoke in time past to the fathers by the prophets" (Hebrews 1:1). God spoke to the prophets, then the prophets spoke to the people. As the original author, God communicated to the human writer in such a way that the writer became the first receptor of the message. God is receptor-oriented in communication, and therefore communicated to the original writer in a way that would be understood as the message was processed through the writer's stew of meaning. God was also able to aid the writer in communicating the message to the secondary receptors, the first readers or listeners. This means that God was dealing with multiple stews of meaning and sometimes had to transcend cultures, such as when Paul and John wrote letters to churches in various places.

To say that we must know the stew of meaning only for the writer or the secondary receptors is to lock that meaning in the distant past that has no meaning for people today. If this is true then we may as well throw the Bible away as a meaningless piece of literature. Denying that God is the author forces us to say that the Bible was written based on purely human ingenuity and concepts; therefore, it can be ignored and discounted as having any substantial moral value. By ignoring the fact that God is the author of the Bible, we take away the book's supernatural element and leave it as a human construct confined to an ancient culture.

The shift in focus from a human writer to God as the author helps us to see the Bible as cross-cultural. God was transcultural in the first communication with the writer. God is not limited by culture. God is outside of human culture and able to speak to all cultures. Since God is receptor-oriented, the communication included all the receptors who would receive the communication, not just the secondary receptors. God gave enough space to the allowable meaning so that the communication would be understood by all cultures.

This does not mean that we should not learn about the historical context of the writers of the Bible. It is helpful to know their history in order to understand how they interpreted the communication from God. After all, God was speaking directly to them; therefore, the communication must have had meaning for them. This is also true as we study others in history who have interpreted the Bible. By knowing the history of the receptors and how they derived meaning, we will have a better understanding of the boundaries of the allowable meaning of the scriptures. The problem is that we have created hermeneutics that focus only on one culture's historical interpretation and have used those culturally specific hermeneutics as the measuring stick for all other interpretations. However, no single culture can determine the meaning for all cultures.

Chapter 8:
A Transcultural
Hermeneutic

What kind of hermeneutic is not culturally centered? As I thought about this question, I asked myself what God wants to communicate through the Bible. God is the author/communicator. The message of the Bible is more than just a list of religious, civil, or moral laws; it is more than just a history lesson or a book on literature appreciation. God wanted to answer specific questions with this book.

Therefore, I believe a simple method is best. After all, God used simple language to reach the masses; there is no reason to believe that God would make it difficult to find the meaning. No matter what genre we are dealing with, we can ask three questions about any part of the Bible. These three questions get to the heart of what God wishes to communicate through the scriptures.

- What does the passage tell me about God?
- What does the passage tell me about people (collectively and as individuals)?
- What does the passage tell me about the relationship between God and humans (collectively and as individuals)?

The answers to the questions help us see the meaning of the passage. But while these questions can be asked about any passage, it does not mean that every passage will provide an answer for all three. Sometimes only one question will be answered.

Truth about God is revealed through the Bible. God designed it that way, so it would make sense that we would find an answer to the first question in much of the Bible. For instance, when we read about Moses meeting God at the burning bush in Exodus 3, we learn that God is holy and to be respected. Passages containing the law tell us that God has determined that there is a right and wrong. We see David expressing characteristics of God through his poetry. Paul declares the truth about Jesus as a basis for his arguments in his letters to the churches.

As we look through the Bible, we are constantly viewing the actions of people. The narratives reveal human actions and desires. The law shows us what people are doing wrong and provides guidelines for living with each other.

The relationship between God and humans is a very important thread throughout the Bible, from Genesis to Revelation. Most of the narratives refer to this interaction as God speaks to someone or takes action for or against someone. The Gospels of the New Testament show God interacting with humans personally. Paul's letters focus on how interaction with Jesus has an impact on our lives as a community.

Using the three simple questions listed above, we can understand a vast amount about the Bible. But other questions can make what we learn more personal. The answers to the previous questions will give us general information, but we cannot stop there if the Bible is to fulfill its goal to speak to individual lives.

- How am I like the person in the narrative?
- Can I identify with the writer's feelings?
- Does this passage relate to a question I have?

As we read through a narrative in the Bible, we should ask if we can identify with one of the characters. Good storytellers always seem to create characters that people can identify with; that is what draws us into the story. God is the ultimate storyteller, and his stories are about real people and their actions, faults, and triumphs. We can ask ourselves if we identify with the person in power or the person who is oppressed or the male or female character. By examining how we are like or different from the character, we will understand the meaning of the narrative. Emotions are powerful things that can drive our minds and bodies. Poetry is an extremely emotional genre in which poets pour out their inward feelings concerning a person or situation. There are some extreme emotions within the Psalms, including anger at God, depression, grief, love for God, and joy. As we read through the Psalms, we must ask ourselves if we can identify with the poet's feelings. If so, then we can hope to find meaning as we look at how the poet processes his feelings.

Most people enjoy stories and many can relate to poetry, but when we come to the letters in the New Testament, many people lose interest. Most of the letters were written to answer questions people had about God or what it means to be a Christian community. As we read them, we should ask if a particular passage touches on a question that we have. When the answer is yes, then we need to pay closer attention to how the writer works through the question to come up with his answer. By identifying our question, we can find meaning from the passage.

None of the six questions highlighted above are tied to a single culture; they are simply human-focused questions that can be asked by anyone. The questions are open enough that anyone can find a meaningful answer within passages of the Bible. What we are doing is learning about ourselves and our situations as we read through the Bible. This hermeneutic is focused on the current receptor, who is the person to whom God desires to speak, rather than on the author or first receptor.

There is no longer a need for God to speak to the writer and first receptors. At each point in history, only the current receptors are important. We cannot, however, disregard previous receptors or their cultural contexts, as they do help us to find the allowable meaning. This is why it is still important to know the context of the biblical authors and any other interpreters we may learn about.

This hermeneutic is rooted in the ancient way of teaching. The instructors of children in ancient societies knew how much a student understood because of the questions they asked, not because of the answers they gave. Anyone can commit something to rote memory without understanding it, but the depth of understanding is found in the questions a student asks a teacher. There have been many occasions in which I did not understand enough to even come up with a question to ask. We see this type of teaching in the Bible. Exodus 13 describes the command to keep the Passover. Verse 14 says that the sons will ask, "What is this?" as they prepare for the feast, and the fathers are to answer. The sons show that they understand that something special is taking place, and the fathers reward that understanding with further information. (See also Exodus

12:26–27.) Questions were also to be asked about the reason for the law God gave to Israel (Deuteronomy 6:20–25). Luke 2:46–47 describes Jesus in the temple, amazing the religious leaders with his questions and answers. Questions are an important part of learning; asking them is just as important, if not more so, than answering them. Is it any wonder that asking questions of God's communication is the best way to interpret it?

However, there is one more very important question we must all ask: *Is there something I need to change about how I view God or people, or how I act, in order to conform to what I have learned from the passage?*

Sometimes the answer to this question is no, as we realize that we are where we need to be. Perhaps the passage gives us hope and strength. The thing we do not want is to be content with finding information in the Bible and not allow it to make a difference within our lives.

Kwame Bediako puts it this way: "We need to allow Scripture to become the interpreter of who we are in the specific concrete sense of who we are in our cultures and traditions."[85] In other words, the meaning we gain from the Bible must make an impact on our lives and be lived out in a concrete manner. The Bible helps to interpret us and our culture as we find the answers to our questions. Justo Gonzalez echoes this sentiment as he states, "It is not so much that we interpret the Bible, as that the Bible interprets us in a radically new and ultimately fulfilling way!"[86] As we find meaning in the Bible passages, we find meaning for and within us. We can see ourselves in a new and better light.

It is important that we do not misunderstand this final question. "We read the Bible, not primarily to find out what we are to do, but to find out who we are and who we are to be."[87] In other words, it is not so much focusing on what we have to change in our life as it is determining who we are now and who we will be when that change occurs. Gonzalez writes, "To read the Bible as a book of guidance, as many do, implies that one is free to make all sorts of choices about one's life."[88] But many people are unable to change their economic or social situations due to the actions of others. However, they can find out who they are in relation to God, which serves as a source of strength and comfort. Therefore, when poor people read the Bible, they do not necessarily find guidance or information; "what they find is rather a world view, and an interpretation of their own predicament, that puts things under a new light and gives them a new sense of worth and hope."[89]

I have known people who are afraid of trying to interpret the Bible for themselves because they are afraid of making mistakes. They hold the

Bible in such regard that they do not want to misrepresent it. I admire that conviction and hold to it myself. But the truth is we are human, and we will make mistakes. Great scholars of the past have made mistakes, and I have made mistakes. The key is that, when we realize that we have made a mistake, we put away the wrong interpretation and substitute it for the correct one. A heretic is a person who will not admit his mistake and change as a result.

Many mistakes are caused by people who simply look for facts and do not allow the Bible to speak to them. If we actually look for the answers to these simple questions, then we will make fewer mistakes, especially if we allow the answers to influence our lives. By holding to the boundaries of the allowable meaning, we will be less likely to step out of bounds. Remember, the Holy Spirit is guiding you. God does not get angry with us when we get something wrong, as long as we are willing to correct it when we are shown the error. We should do our homework and learn how others have interpreted passages and about the original cultures of the Bible. But we should not be so caught up in that process that we miss the true intent of the Bible, i.e., God communicating truth to us for our benefit.

Some people might be wondering if I advocate getting rid of all other hermeneutics and just using this one. I am not proposing that at all. In fact, I believe that would be the worst mistake we could make. There is nothing wrong with a culturally centered hermeneutic as long as we recognize it as such and that other culturally based hermeneutics are just as viable. I am simply trying to help people regain the perspective that God wants to speak to them directly through the Bible in a way that is culturally relevant to them. The Bible is not bound by culture, but we are, and the Bible allows for that. This is the message I am trying to promote.

CHAPTER 9:
JESUS'S HERMENEUTIC

IN THINKING ABOUT THIS hermeneutic, I decided to go to the source. I wanted to know how Jesus interpreted the Bible. If his interpretation was completely different than my proposal, then I would have to change my thinking. To get a feel for the method he used, I turned to the book of Matthew in which Jesus quotes the Old Testament twenty-two times.

THE TEMPTATION

Satan tempted Jesus in the desert (Matthew 4). He tempted Jesus three times, and Jesus answered all three with quotations from the scriptures. The three temptations and answers deal with the relationship between God and humans. It is interesting that Jesus did not exert his power as God to create a new scripture for this circumstance; instead, he relied on the scriptures that were and are fully accessible to humans.

Satan first asked Jesus to satisfy his hunger by creating bread from stones. Jesus responded in verse 4 by quoting Deuteronomy 8:3: "Man shall not live by bread alone, but by every word that proceeds from the mouth of God." Jesus reflects back on this verse, which was spoken to the people of Israel while they were wandering in the desert. It is directly connected to God providing manna to keep the Israelites from starving, but that food is not enough. People must live on the words of God. Jesus seems to interpret this passage to mean that our relationship with God is as important or as natural as eating. For Jesus, this passage answers the question: What is the relationship between God and humans, collectively and as individuals? Satan wanted Jesus to end his relationship with God and go off on his own, but Jesus knew better.

During the second temptation, the devil took Jesus to the top of the temple and told him to jump because God would catch and protect him. Satan actually quoted from the Bible to prove his point: "For He shall give His angels charge over you, to keep you in all your ways. In their hands they shall bear you up, lest you dash your foot against a stone" (Psalm 91:11–12). However, the devil committed a cardinal error in his use of scripture; he pulled it out of context. The passage describes a person who is devoted to God and who wants to live in the way God intended. It does not describe someone who simply does whatever he wants without asking if it is what God wants him to do. Jesus spotted this error and quoted Deuteronomy 6:16 in rebuttal: "You shall not tempt the Lord your God." That verse is about following the ways of God and not trying to go it on your own. Once again the nature of the relationship is answered in this passage. Indeed, both passages speak about having a strong relationship with God that does not include testing the boundaries by doing something on your own and expecting God to bail you out.

In the third temptation, according to Matthew, Satan asked Jesus to worship him; in exchange he would become the ruler of the world. Jesus responded, "You shall fear the Lord your God and serve Him" (Deuteronomy 6:13), which is part of a passage that describes how the Israelites might react if they were given the Promised Land and houses and vineyards without working for them. Jesus determined that this passage was about our relationship with God, which should not be forgotten when things are going well. To have the world is not wrong, but to receive it from Satan and to worship Satan instead of God is definitely wrong.

In each of these three quotations, Jesus asked about the relationship between God and humans. He found the answers in the scriptures, without taking them out of context or twisting their meaning. Jesus used the plain, simple meaning of each text to make his point to the devil, who was trying to end the relationship between Jesus and the Father.

THE SERMON ON THE MOUNT

Matthew 5 is the first of the three chapters that comprise the Sermon on the Mount. It is the longest recorded sermon given by Jesus and appears to be a part of his stock message, or stump speech, which he frequently gave. Parts of this sermon appear in other places in the Gospels and in other locales besides the mountain. In chapter 5, Jesus quotes from four passages of the Hebrew Scriptures.

The first quote is in Matthew 5:21–26. It is taken from Exodus 20:13 and Deuteronomy 5:17 and is from the Ten Commandments: "You shall not murder." People had been saying that only those who committed the physical act of murder would face final judgment. Jesus responded there was more to a violation than a physical action. In effect, he was asking, "What does this quotation say about humans, collectively and as individuals?" The answer is that there is something in human nature that allows evil to take root and grow. Human relationships can be as harmed by internal feelings and attitudes as they can by exterior actions. Killing someone ends one's relationship with that person. Emotions like hate and envy that take root in people can also end relationships and deserve the same judgment as the physical taking of a life. Such actions can also harm our relationship with God, which is another question the passage in Matthew answers. When we wrong someone and do not try to make it right, we hurt our relationship with God (Matthew 5:23–24). Jesus saw this passage as answering at least two of the questions from our hermeneutic. He did not say to the people, "This is what it said in the ancient culture, and this is what it now says." He simply stated what it had always meant. It is interesting to note that Jesus did not lay aside the cultural idiom about being in danger of judgment. Instead he showed how that idiom related to the passage the people were quoting.

The second quotation is in Matthew 5:27–30. Again, Jesus quoted from the Ten Commandments: "You shall not commit adultery" (Exodus 20:14, Deuteronomy 5:18), and then asked questions related to God's relationship with humans. People allow the seed of lust to take root in their minds and lives, an attitude that often leads to the action of adultery. Such inward attitudes harm the relationship between God and humans, which is what Jesus is speaking about when he talks about hell. They keep us from having a right relationship with God. It is better to avoid satisfying the lusts of the body and maintain a strong relationship with God.

In both of these cases, Jesus directed people to find answers in scripture. He understood that there was an underlying reason that God placed boundaries on human behavior. By using the example of the corrupted seeds, he showed the true meaning of the passages he quoted. What do the Ten Commandments tell us about people? They tell us that we are capable of causing harm to ourselves and others because we allow corrupted thoughts and attitudes to take root, grow, and bear fruit. Jesus's interpretation shows people how to avoid breaking the Commandments.

The third quotation is found in Matthew 5:38–42 and is one that many people are familiar with today: "an eye for an eye and a tooth for a tooth," taken from Exodus, Leviticus, and Deuteronomy. In Exodus 21:24, the passage refers to what should happen if a person hurts a pregnant woman during a fight, and she gives birth prematurely. If any harm comes to the woman or the child, there should be repayment in kind. In other words, if the baby is deformed, then the person who caused the early birth should be deformed as well. Leviticus 24:20 speaks about a person deliberately disfiguring someone else and receiving the same treatment. Deuteronomy 19:21 describes a person who has brought false witness against another person and suffers a similar punishment. God enacted this to keep people from using the court system as a way to hurt others. Asking what this says about humans, Jesus's answer was that humans are prone to revenge. The "eye for an eye" concept was meant to keep people from going too far in their revenge. You could not kill a person for hurting your hand. Jesus exposes this meaning as he tells the people to not seek revenge at all. People have to be willing to give of themselves and their property rather than seeking revenge or profit. Revenge is a seed wrapped in the shell of anger and bitterness, which can easily take root and cause physical harm.

The final scripture quotation is found in Matthew 5:43–48. He quotes from Leviticus 19:18: "love your neighbor as yourself." The next part advises against hating your enemies, which is not a quotation from scripture but an idiom from the culture. Jesus's interpretation of this scripture answers all three questions associated with our hermeneutic. Show love to all, for everyone is our neighbor even if we don't get along with all people at all times. How we treat other people reflects on our relationship with God and what we think about God. God loves everyone, even those who hate him. If we do not do the same, then we are not displaying the true nature of God. The passage in Leviticus says that we should leave revenge to God. As a being who loves everyone, God, unlike most humans, can give proper punishment without turning it into a vendetta.

DEBATES WITH RELIGIOUS LEADERS

Jesus had many debates with the religious leaders of his time. These people knew the scriptures very well and had their own interpretations of them. Jesus sometimes pointed to familiar scriptures and told the leaders to learn the true meaning. One example can be found in Matthew 9:13.

The religious leaders had condemned Jesus for eating with the outcasts of society, the tax collectors and sinners. Jesus quoted Hosea 6:6, "I desire mercy and not sacrifice," and told the leaders to learn what it meant. Simply put, God values the inward trait of mercy over the outward act of sacrifice. People who have a relationship with God should exhibit his trait of showing mercy. The religious leaders were not showing mercy; they were showering condemnation and judgment toward people who were sinners in their eyes.

The next short debate occurs in Matthew 12:1–8. Jesus, his disciples, and the religious leaders were walking through a field on the Sabbath. The disciples were hungry and began to take some of the heads of grain and eat them. To the religious leaders, this was harvesting grain, which defied the law prohibiting work on the Sabbath. They rebuked Jesus for allowing his disciples to do this. They believed that if Jesus was presenting himself as a religious leader, he should obey the Sabbath. In response, Jesus related a story from 1 Samuel 21:1–6: David was on the run from King Saul. He and his men needed supplies. The priest offered bread, which only he was supposed to eat, to David, who used it to feed his men as they fled from Saul. Jesus pointed to Old Testament law: priests can offer sacrifices on the Sabbath even though it is a day of rest. Jesus again quoted from Hosea 6:6: God created the law to help people, not to hurt them. God is merciful. If he sees someone who is hungry, he wants to feed that person, even if it breaks the law. God desires merciful action instead of adherence to the law, which causes inaction. Once again, Jesus used the scriptures to display a truth about God and the relationship between God and humans.

Further on, in Matthew 12:38–42, the religious leaders told Jesus they wanted a sign that proved that he was the Messiah. Jesus responded by referring to the stories of Jonah and the queen of Sheba (1 Kings 10:1–13) in the Old Testament. In Jonah 3, the people of Nineveh understood the characteristic of God's holiness. They repented their sins and relied on God's mercy that they would not be destroyed. The queen understood God's ability to give gifts such as wisdom and saw the proof in Solomon. The people of Nineveh and the queen of Sheba understood the relationship between people and God. Jesus pointed out that if these people, who were not Jewish, understood when God was doing something, then the Jewish religious leaders should understand enough about God to know what he could do and when he was at work. Once again, Jesus pointed to a truth about God and the relationship he has with humans.

Another confrontation occurs in Matthew 15:1–9. The religious leaders accused Jesus's disciples of failing to follow the tradition of washing their hands before eating. Jesus responded by quoting the fifth commandment, "Honor your father and mother" (Exodus 20:12, Deuteronomy 5:16), and then Exodus 21:17, "He who curses his father or mother shall surely be put to death." He then said, "These people draw near to Me with their mouth, and honor me with their lips, but their heart is far from me" (Isaiah 29:13). Finally, he turned to what we learn about humans, saying the scriptures show that people, specifically these religious leaders, are deceitful when they find loopholes in the laws, even the laws of God. People can seem to obey the law but be far from a relationship with God.

The religious leaders decided to test Jesus, so they asked him about the legality of divorce for any reason (Matthew 19:3–9). Jesus responded, "He who made them at the beginning made them male and female" (Genesis 1:27; 5:2), and added "For this reason a man shall leave his father and mother and be joined to his wife, and the two shall become one flesh" (Genesis 2:24). Jesus wanted the religious leaders to see the difference between God and people, who are prone to changing their mind about relationships. God, however, is not. Those who truly follow God take relationships seriously and do not discard people on a whim. In other words, they do not divorce for "just any reason," such as, because one's wife burned the supper. There has to be a real, significant, breach of the relationship by the other person to cause a divorce.

During his final week of ministry, Jesus entered Jerusalem and turned over the tables of the money changers in the temple (Matthew 21:12–13), who were taking advantage of people and cheating them for profit. Jesus defended his actions by quoting Isaiah 56:7 and Jeremiah 7:11. Our relationship with God should be based on prayer and worship, not economics. People try to use things of God for their own benefit, stealing from God and tarnishing his character. Once again, Jesus used simple phrases to show the character of humans and their relationship with God.

Later in the temple, Jesus healed people, and the children got excited. They called Jesus the "Son of David," which was a term used for the king of Israel and the Messiah. The children's words irritated the religious leaders who confronted Jesus about it. Jesus replied by quoting Psalm 8:2. His point was that children and innocent people have a pure relationship with God; they understand when God is at work around them. The religious leaders were intentionally blind to the truth that the children saw so clearly.

When he debated with the religious leaders in the temple, Jesus related a series of parables, which were against the religious leaders. At the end, he quoted Psalms 118:22–23, "The stone which the builders rejected has become the chief cornerstone. This was the Lord's doing; it is marvelous in our eyes." The religious leaders had looked at the cornerstone of God's plan for the redemption of humans and rejected it as a piece of scrap, unworthy to be placed in the building. Jesus was saying that God—and not people—decides who and what is important. God is much more intelligent than humans, whose intelligence is diminished by bigotry and self-interest.

A sect of Judaism, the Sadducees, did not believe in the resurrection of the dead. They decided to test Jesus by making fun of this idea (Matthew 22:23–33). They proposed an improbable situation in which a woman married seven brothers, in keeping with the Law of Moses, and then dies. Which brother, they asked, would she be married to during the resurrection? Jesus answered that they were mistaken that there would be such a relationship as marriage during the resurrection. He challenged them by quoting Exodus 3:6 and 3:15. God is the God of the living, not the dead. For God to be the God of Abraham, Isaac, and Jacob after they had departed this world, they must still be alive. Jesus used a common and revered phrase from the Old Testament to reveal a great truth about God.

Right after this exchange another religious leader, who was well versed in the Law of Moses, asked Jesus to weigh in on the most debated topic in Judaism. Everyone wanted to know which commandment was the most important (Matthew 22:35–40). Jesus responded by quoting from Deuteronomy 6:5 and Leviticus 19:18. The most important part of living is to love God and other humans. All the other laws are derived from showing how these actions are to be exhibited. Since Jesus put loving God first, it seems that it is difficult to love other people if we do not love God.

Finally, in this heated exchange, Jesus took the offensive (Matthew 22:41–45). He quoted Psalm 110:1 to the religious leaders: "The Lord said to my Lord, sit at my right hand." This passage was written by King David, who was the greatest of all the kings in Israel. Yet a person who would become king after him would be David's Lord. The king to come would be a descendant of David, yet he would be David's Lord? Jesus asked the religious leaders what that passage told them about the coming

Christ. The answer Jesus was looking for is that the Christ is God in the flesh. Jesus was teaching the religious leaders a truth about God that they did not want to accept.

OTHER QUOTATIONS IN MATTHEW

There is one other time in Matthew where Jesus quoted from scripture as he was teaching. A rich young man seeking religious advice asked Jesus which laws had to be kept in order to reach heaven (Matthew 19:16–22). Jesus responded by quoting Exodus 20:12–16 and Deuteronomy 5:16–20, which are part of the Ten Commandments, and also Leviticus 19:18, the passage about loving your neighbor. The young man thought that he had done everything, but Jesus showed him that he held too tightly to his riches. The young man had failed to love his neighbors, as we often do, because he did not recognize the plight of the poor or show true concern for them. It seems to be a human trait to look out for ourselves first and ignore the plight of others, which is why God had to give us the law in the first place—to show us what we were lacking.

The only other quotation from scripture by Jesus found in Matthew is during the crucifixion when he quoted Psalm 22:1: "My God, My God, why have You forsaken Me?" (27:46). This quotation shows the ugliness associated with the payment for sin, as Jesus no longer felt the presence of God. This is the position humans will end up in for eternity if they do not accept God into the core of their lives.

ANALYSIS OF JESUS'S HERMENEUTIC

As we study the quotations Jesus used from the Old Testament, we find that he used legal, poetic, narrative, and prophetic passages to answer a variety of questions. Yet, in effect, he was always answering the same three questions. Each time, Jesus relayed a truth about God, humans, or the relationship between God and humans, which is consistent with the hermeneutic I have proposed.

Jesus did not take the scriptures out of their literary context to get them to mean what he wanted. The people to whom he was speaking had an easier time understanding his point, because they could associate the quotation with the original passage. Jesus used texts with which everyone would have been familiar, such as he did in the Sermon on the Mount. However, he felt more at liberty with the religious leaders, who would have known the entire Old Testament, and used more obscure quotes and fragments with them, such as Hosea 6:6 (in Matthew 9:13), and Isaiah

29:13 (in Matthew 15:1–9). When Jesus turned over the money changers' tables, he quoted from Isaiah and Jeremiah. The Isaiah quotation came from a passage that discussed Gentiles ability to pray at the temple. The tables would have been set up in the outer court, the Court of the Gentiles, which was reserved as a place where they could pray, and not for economic transactions. The Jeremiah quotation came from a passage in which God disciplined religious leaders for their oppression of the poor. The money changers had profited by inflating the rates that governed the exchange of the people's money for the temple coin, which was the only money that could be used for offerings or the buying of sacrifices. Because Jesus retained the context, the religious leaders were well aware what he was condemning. Retaining the integrity of the literary context is important when we interpret the Bible.

Jesus always assumed the author of the Bible was God and therein lies the authority of the words he quoted. He saw the message of the Bible as directed to the people and situation he was dealing with at the time. This helps me to see that my shift from viewing the human writers as the authors, to viewing them as the first receptors, is legitimate. It also helps to solidify the concept that the Bible was originally and intentionally designed for multiple receptors, including the writer and his initial readers (the secondary receptors).

Even though Jesus was quoting from passages written 400 to 1,500 years earlier, he did not see the Bible as chained to past cultures. He did not stand there and say, "It meant this for them in the old days, but this is how we should understand it in our current culture." Remember all of the cultural changes that had taken place since the writing of the quoted passages. The people of Israel had been nomads in the desert, became a nation and a world power, and finally ended up exiled and scattered all over the world. After the last word of the Old Testament was written, Israel was conquered by the Greek and Romans and exposed to their cultures. Yet Jesus assumed that the scriptures spoke directly to the culture with which he was dealing. This shows that Jesus saw the Bible as relevant for all times and cultures.

After reviewing the method Jesus used to interpret scripture, I am more confident in my proposal. The Bible is not chained to an ancient culture and, in fact, was created to reach all cultures. The three questions I presented in chapter 8 are accurate and were used by Jesus to give meaning to the Old Testament. We can rest easier knowing that this method is consistent with Jesus's actions and his handling of the scriptures.

CHAPTER 10:
USING THE TRANSCULTURAL
HERMENEUTIC

I WOULD LIKE TO close this section by giving you an idea of how the simple transcultural hermeneutic works. We will look at passages of legal text, poetry, and a letter. Please look them up and read them in the translation of your choice. This is a part of the hermeneutic. As we look at each passage, we will ask the three basic questions:

- What does it say about God?
- What does it say about people, collectively and as individuals?
- What does it say about the relationship between God and people, collectively and as individuals?

We will also ask the three follow-up questions, when appropriate:

- How am I like the person in the narrative?
- Can I identify with the poet's feelings?
- Does this passage relate to a question I have?

Finally, we will ask the most important question about each passage: *Is there something I should change about how I view or act toward God or people in order to conform to what I have learned from the passage?*

I hope this will help you see that the Bible is not confined to a single culture and can speak to you directly.

LEVITICUS 19:9–10

This passage is part of the law that was given to us through Moses. It is found in the context of moral laws; the chapter begins with God calling people to be holy and then gives specific laws as guidance toward that goal. This passage talks about how farmers are to harvest their fields.

What does it say about God?
God cares about the poor. We can see that this is true by verifying it through other scripture. Remember, the Bible helps to set the boundaries for interpretation. By looking at other passages, such as Jeremiah 5:26–29 and Amos 5:10–15, we learn that God punished Israel for oppressing, instead of helping, the poor.

What does it say about people?
So many people failed to help those who were less fortunate that a law was needed to force them to do what was morally correct. Think about it. If people do something naturally, they do not have to be told to do it. People get wrapped up in their own problems and forget that others may need help. A little reminder does not hurt.

In this case, the law applied to individuals who owned land. At that time, most of the people would have been farmers, and all would own land after they entered the Promised Land. While the law was phrased for individuals, it was a reminder to the entire population to be aware of the poor and help them in their struggles to sustain life.

What does it say about the relationship between God and humans?
The passage's final phrase shows us that God is like a parent, demanding that his children do what he says because he knows what is best for the children. God is in the position of authority over humans. Therefore, he has the right and responsibility to make laws that will benefit them.

Is there something I should change about how I view or act toward God or people in order to conform to what I have learned from the passage?
After reading this passage, think about what you are not doing for those who are less fortunate. For example, many people give financial or in-kind assistance to charities that help the poor. In the United States, some food

corporations donate to food banks. If someone is in a position to give to or help another person, then he should do so.

But what if you are the person who needs help? Interestingly, this law is not about a handout; it is about a hand up. The poor still had to harvest the grain themselves, which gave them a sense of self-worth because they worked for what they received. Are you trying to find work while you get help from the government or a charity? Are you looking forward to the day when you will not have to receive help, but will be a person who can give help?

Perhaps you do not have much money and are barely getting by. You cannot afford to give money to others, but you are finally at a point where you no longer need assistance. Maybe you can use your voice or your time to promote laws, businesses, or charities that help the less fortunate. Think of some practical ways to help others.

You might also ask what your view of God is. In your opinion, is God supposed to give you whatever you want, whenever you want it? Or does God help you as you work and try to use your resources wisely? Some people place the full responsibility for their care on God, while others take on all the responsibility. It is actually a combination of the two, with both sides having some responsibility. The farmer plants and harvests the grain, and God allows it to grow. In my relationship with God, what is my role when it comes to providing the necessities of life for my family?

Psalm 139:1–6
The book of Psalms is the Hebrew book of poetry. This passage is from a song written by King David.

What does it say about God?
This passage tells us that God knows us better than we know ourselves. God is not some distant being, far away and outside our universe. He is up close and has an intimate relationship with each and every person.

What does it say about people?
The love and closeness of God is a mystery that humans cannot fully understand.

What does it say about the relationship between God and humans?

Even when we do not feel the presence of God, he is still there with us. We have a close, physical, and intimate relationship with him that is deeper than any human relationship could ever be.

Can I identify with the poet's feelings?
The poet seems to focus on the presence of God. At times, I need to remind myself that God is with me. In times of sorrow, or if I am having a bad day, it may seem like God is far from me. I can remind myself that God is not absent, that he knows what I am going through. I think that may be what David is doing with this psalm. He is having a bad time and reminding himself that God has not abandoned him.

Is there something I should change about how I view or act toward God or people in order to conform to what I have learned from the passage?
I need to spend more time remembering that God is present and knows me better than I know myself. When I get discouraged, I should focus on the presence of God in my life, like David did.

1 Corinthians 12:12–14
This passage is from a letter from the Apostle Paul to the local church in the ancient city of Corinth. These verses fall in the middle of a discussion on the unity of the church.

What does it say about people?
People have a tendency to divide themselves from others. We use race, culture, ethnicity, economic status, gender, and other things to distinguish ourselves and make ourselves feel superior. This can lead to oppression or rejection of other people or groups.

What does it say about God?
God does not make distinctions among people based on human-derived categories. All are equal in the sight of God, and all are worthy of love.

What does it say about the relationship between God and humans?
All who enter into a relationship with God through Jesus are equal in God's eyes. They are all loved. God wants everyone to enter into that relationship (2 Peter 3:9).

Does this passage relate to a question I have?

Diversity within the church is a big issue. If all people are equal within the global church, is it wrong to have churches that are segregated economically or racially? Obviously it is wrong to exclude any member of the global church from a local congregation due to his ethnic background, gender, economic standing, or any of the other areas we use to distinguish ourselves from others. However it does not seem to be wrong to have a congregation in which only Spanish, or Chinese, or some other language is spoken, or one that has a particular cultural bent, as long as all are free to join.

Is there something I should change about how I view or act toward God or people in order to conform to what I have learned from the passage?
Paul recognized diversity but focused on equality. Perhaps I need to do more to promote equality within the church. If we promote equality, then diversity will take care of itself. Instead of trying to introduce more minorities to the congregation, maybe it would be better to truly view the minority group within the church as equals. That seems to be a better strategy to me, to draw people in rather than drag them in. Viewing people as equal displays love, while striving for diversity displays tolerance. I would rather love than be tolerant.

CONCLUSION
I hope you find these examples helpful. I cannot stress enough that my goal is not to discount other forms of hermeneutics. I am trying to simplify the hermeneutic and make it more transcultural instead of a slave to any particular culture. Admittedly, these examples display my cultural bent, and your answers will display your cultural bent, but that does not make either set of answers better than another.

SECTION III:
THE CHURCH AND YOU

CHAPTER 11: THE CHURCH

Imagine you are a leader within the new, first-century community of believers in Christ. Jesus has now ascended into heaven, and you are the spiritual leader and guide of his followers. Where do you turn for truth about Jesus? How do you prove to others that what you are teaching about Jesus is true? You can rely on only one source: the Bible.

Today, the Bible remains an integral part of the global transcultural organism that is the church. It is a unifying pillar in doctrine, teaching, and spiritual renewal. The scriptures are known to all followers of Christ. Without the written words of God, we could not be certain of the truth about Jesus and our relationship with him and each other. The church is Christ centered, but our knowledge of Jesus comes from the Bible. Remove the scriptures from the church, and you will be left with people's ideas and whims about Jesus without a shred of solid evidence to support them. Remove the pillar of scripture from the church, and it will soon collapse into a collection of myth and fairytales.

THE BIBLE IS A PILLAR OF THE CHURCH

From the very beginning, the Bible has been a pillar of the church community's culture. The first thing Jesus did with his disciples after the resurrection was to go through the Old Testament. He pointed out the scriptures that spoke about the Christ and his mission (Luke 24:27, 44–47). Peter used scripture to prove Jesus was the Christ during his first sermon in Acts 2. Later in Acts 6:1–7, we find the apostles studying the scriptures to strengthen the church theologically and spiritually. At the Jerusalem Council, described in Acts 15, the leaders of the fledgling church discussed the admission of Gentiles without making them first convert to

Judaism. James quoted from scripture to end the debate and allow Gentiles into the church without prior conditions (Acts 15:15–17).

Paul told his protégé Timothy to preach the scriptures as the basis for doctrine and exhortation (2 Timothy 4:2). Those who followed Paul and the other apostles did the same. Clement of Alexandria (153–217 CE) emphatically stated, "But those who are ready to toil in the most excellent pursuits will not desist from the search after truth till they get the demonstration from the Scriptures themselves."[90] Clement was saying that, when it comes to truth about God, humans, and the relationship between God and humans, the basis for knowledge is found in the scriptures. He also stated, "For we have, as the source of teaching, the Lord, both by the prophets, the Gospel, and the blessed apostles, 'in diverse manners and at sundry times,' leading from the beginning of knowledge to the end."[91] Clement believed that truth would not change; therefore, the truth in the Bible would not change and could be used as the source of teaching. In other writings, he appealed to those who had interpreted the scriptures in the past and battled the heretical doctrines promoted by people who relied on Greek philosophy rather than the scriptures for their truth. These people reached conclusions that went beyond the boundaries of allowable meaning.

The Apostle Paul leveled the same warning to the Galatians, i.e., not to allow others to preach a type of Gospel that did not agree with the scriptures (Galatians 1:6–12). Justin Martyr also showed his reliance on the scriptures when he defended the faith to Trypho: "But if I quote frequently Scriptures, and so many of them, referring to this point, and ask you to comprehend them, you are hard-hearted in the recognition of the mind and will of God."[92] Justin considered Trypho to be stubborn because he did not acknowledge what the scriptures plainly said. He referred to quoting from many scriptures, which means he believed the Bible was the best interpreter of itself, which is one of the points for finding the allowable meaning.

The early church often held councils or synods during which representatives from various congregations discussed key issues connected to doctrine or practices. These councils stressed the importance of scripture within local congregations, whether they met on Saturday in honor of the Sabbath, or on Sunday in honor of the resurrection. The Council in Antioch assumed that scripture reading was a natural part of meetings of congregations, referring to participants as "All who enter the church of God and hear the Holy Scriptures."[93] This assumption would not have been valid if scripture reading had not been a familiar part of their services. Keep in mind these people represented congregations from all over Europe, Africa, Persia, and Asia Minor. It is obvious that this was a universal action within the churches.

In 781, a monument was erected in China in honor of the Nestorians, Christians from Persia. Samuel Moffet notes that on this monument, "There is little emphasis on the centrality of Scripture, which was so basic a premise of Nestorian theological studies in Persia."[94] The church in Persia was very much focused on the scripture. When its missionaries went to China, scripture was still in their vision but perhaps not as much as it had been in Persia.

Today the Bible is an integral part of the church service and church life. Sermons are based on scripture passages and are presented to the congregation. Outside the regular meeting times, many church communities schedule Bible study groups at the church itself or the homes of members. On the radio, pastors preach and teach from the scriptures. The Bible is still looked to for answers on any topic or situation within the lives of a congregation or individual member.

THE TRANSCULTURAL CHURCH

Many people do not realize how transcultural the church was and is. They focus on their own congregation or community, and do not pay attention to the broader picture. To get a proper picture of the church and Jesus, we need to move beyond our current, local experiences. Let us take a quick look at how diverse the early church was.

The church originally was commanded by Jesus to be transcultural (Matthew 28:18–20, Luke 24:47, Acts 1:8); therefore, it was transcultural from its beginnings. This command was a geographical extension of Jesus's ministry, which was also transcultural. Jesus stayed within the confines of Palestine and ministered to the rich, including Nicodemus, Joseph of Arimathaea, Zacchaeus, and some of the women who followed him. He ministered to the poor and the outcasts, such as tax collectors, women, and lepers. Jesus did not distinguish among the races, working with Jews, Gentiles (such as the centurion), and Samaritans. Politics or philosophical differences did not matter to him either; he presented his message to those who held strongly to the Jewish culture and to those who flocked toward Greek culture. Galilee had more Greek cities than any other area inside Israel and was looked down on by most of the Hebrews. However, that was where Jesus came from and where he spent most of his three-year ministry. It seems only natural that Jesus would command the church, his ministers and representatives on earth, to be transcultural as well and to fulfill the promise of the Old Testament to bless all the nations of the earth (Genesis 12:3).

Even going to just the Jewish communities would have required extending the mission out of Israel and into the rest of the world. The seeds had been sown much earlier through the Diaspora.

A KEY TO DIVERSITY AND MISSIONS

There are people who earnestly want to help their local churches become culturally and ethnically diverse. This has been a concern since the church's very beginning. In first-century Israel, two cultures consistently fought against each other. Hellenistic Jews liked the culture promoted by the Greeks and incorporated it into their lifestyles. Orthodox Jews were more likely to adhere to the old ways. For example, it would be like an East Asian nation in which some of the population adopted Western culture and the rest retained traditional Asian culture.

In Acts 6, we see these two cultures collide within the Church of Jerusalem. Apparently every day, some type of support was given to church widows because they did not have adequate means of support. A problem arose when people noticed that the Hebrew widows were given preferential treatment over the Hellenistic widows. Complaints of discrimination abounded, and the apostles had to step in to solve the problem.

The Church of Jerusalem solved the situation by selecting seven people to dispense the daily support to the widows. Interestingly, all the men had Greek names, which means they were Hellenistic Jews. Apparently, the congregation had no problem placing the minority culture into a position of leadership within the church. There is no mention of these servants, or deacons, showing bias against the Hebrew widows. The church grew after this decision.

Two of these men obtained greater prominence. Stephen became the first recorded martyr, and Philip became an evangelist to those outside of the Jewish culture. Philip witnessed to people in Samaria who had experienced racial discrimination from the Jews, and he witnessed to an Ethiopian who had converted to Judaism but was still considered a Gentile. Perhaps because he was a member of the minority population himself, Philip was able to understand the suffering that accompanied prejudice and have compassion for these people. Could local churches today benefit by having leaders from minority groups? In other words, if a congregation has a large population of upper-income people and a small percentage of lower-income members, wouldn't it benefit by having people from the lower-income group as leaders? The people of the Jerusalem church believed that would be the case, and it helped the church to grow at a crucial time in its development.

According to the Jews of the first century, there were two types of people in the world; Jews and Gentiles. This had more to do with race than culture. While the early church struggled over whether people had to convert to Judaism to become Christian, the question was really deeper than that. The Jewish race was God's chosen people. This was a part of their cultural and ethnic identity. They had a hard time letting go of that distinction and allowing Gentiles into the fold.

As discussed above, Acts 15 relates the story of what happened when Gentiles were allowed into the church without first converting to Judaism. The leaders asked Gentiles to observe a few basic rules, so that Jews would not turn away from the church. All of the arguments in chapter 15 are not so much about Judaism as they are about the Gentiles also being chosen by God. The argument was more racial than religious. Through this decision the church was able to become more diverse, and continued to grow. This is what God had planned all along (Acts 15:13–18).

While many different factors contribute to the lack of diversity within the modern church, I believe one of the biggest factors is the way we view the Bible. We have already discussed the fact that the Bible is a pillar of the church—the source for doctrine, encouragement, and spiritual renewal. Many Christians fail to see the Bible as cross-cultural. They believe it is tied to an ancient culture or, perhaps, that it can be interpreted only through the lens of a single modern culture. If the pillar is not cross-cultural, how can we expect the church that relies on it to be transcultural or ethnically diverse? The Bible must be taught as a cross-cultural text, so that the diversity within it can be modeled within the modern church.

No single culture or ethnic group has the monopoly on the Bible or its interpretation. Being Eurocentric is fine if you are a European or hold to European culture and thought, but it is not good for the rest of the world. We must be able to interpret the Bible in such a way that it enters our world, our culture; otherwise it cannot accomplish its goal of changing our lives. To demand that the Bible be interpreted only through the lens of a single culture is to strip it of its ability to speak to people outside that culture, because it can no longer enter their world. To avoid this, some missionaries attempt to bring the people they are ministering to into their culture. In other words, we are back to the question presented to the Jerusalem council: does someone have to adopt a completely different culture to become a Christian or understand the Bible?

When we view the Bible as a book from a single culture, or interpret it only through a particular culture's view, we skew the way we view the church. We begin to see our culturally specific interpretation of the Bible as *the* pillar of the global church, instead of *a* pillar of our local congregation. We then try to force other congregations to adopt our culturally specific interpretation. And if they do not, then we feel that they are not part of the true global church.

A person's definition of the church then would be that his culture is the focal point. Congregations from other cultures would be just missions of the church, whose members would have to be taught how to interpret the Bible "correctly" through the eyes of the primary culture. That explains why many missionaries stay in one place and never move beyond the congregation they start. Instead of allowing the people to use their own culture and interpretative methods, they feel the need to change that culture, which takes a lot of time and effort.

Single Culture View of the Church

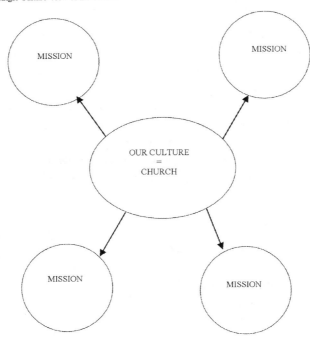

If we see the Bible as a cross-cultural text that is able to speak to all cultures, then we get a different view of the church and our definition changes. We define the church as a global entity composed of all the congregations of the world, each one equal to all others. No single culture has the monopoly on the pillar of truth we call the Bible or its interpretation. Missionaries with a cross-cultural view of the Bible do not spend time trying to convert people into their cultures or create "mission" congregations. The church is viewed as one global, transcultural organism that is expanded by missions into other cultures. Ethnic and cultural differences are welcome and make the church richer without causing strife and prejudice. The growth of the church is not hindered by the need for people to conform to a particular culture in order to understand the Bible. Therefore, the Gospel is planted into various cultures faster and easier.

Transcultural View of the Church

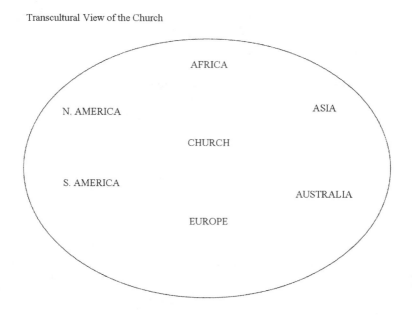

Without a doubt, the church is transcultural. In the book of Revelation, the Apostle John wrote about his vision of heaven, which was given to him by God. He said that he saw a great multitude consisting of all nations and cultures who were praising Jesus and the Father (John 7:9). Almost all interpreters see this as a picture of the church in heaven. We need to relate this heavenly vision to the Lord's model prayer. Jesus told us to pray that God's will would be done on the earth as it is in heaven (Matthew 6:10). If the picture of the church in heaven is transcultural, then surely we should do everything we can to see that it is transcultural here on earth. God has provided the cross-cultural text to accomplish this task, but it will take people who properly view the Bible in this way.

Whether a culture communicates more through an oral or written word is a main area of concern when providing a cross-cultural venue for the message of the Bible. Some cultures communicate orally, even if a group of people has immigrated to a place that is mainly concerned with written words. They will retain their predisposition to oral communication, even though they are surrounded by others who prefer to write. For example, someone coming from a society where lessons are learned through storytellers might prefer to communicate via word of mouth. If that person moved to a society that was dependent on the written word, he still would be more likely to learn better through oral communication.

Many of the world's cultures are reliant on the written word, but let us not shy away from oral traditions. After all, the Bible began within an oral culture, and all cultures were primarily oral until the invention of the printing press. People with oral cultures should be able to learn from and embrace the Bible as much as those who concentrate on written language.

The text of the Bible can be easily transferred back to an oral form. The narrative portions and the Psalms are the easiest to transfer; the letters of the New Testament were originally meant to be read to congregations. This must not be ignored as the church uses and presents information from the Bible. It would be beneficial for churches to promote reading from and listening to the Bible during church services, which would help connect the message to both styles of communication and learning.

A group of people studying how local church congregations could become more transcultural "found that narrative frameworks are helpful when coming to understand and practice being the people of God as a diverse community. Narrative not only asks 'Who am I?' but 'Who is God?' and 'Who are we in God?'"[95] The congregations studied are taking the Bible and making it a part of their lives through cultural interpretation. The narrative framework helps them realize that they are a part of God's continuing story of redemption. They are able to see how their culture plays a part in the global story as well as in their local heritage. It is interesting that the congregations are being asked same questions that we asked about the scriptures: Who am I? (What does the Bible say about humans?) Who is God? (What does it say about God?) Who are we in God? (What does it say about the relationship between God and humans?) While the meaning of scripture can be very personal, it is also corporate. When a congregation asks these questions about scripture, members will find the answers and meaning for their entire group.

It seems obvious that the Bible is a pillar for the church. It is also clear that the Bible is a key to diversity within the church, and it is the reason missions to other cultures are possible.

CHAPTER 12:
WHAT ABOUT YOU?

IT IS IMPORTANT THAT we end this book by showing you what this really means for you. First, what does the Bible say about the importance of scripture for the individual? If the Bible does not stress that individuals need to read and understand scripture for themselves, then maybe it is not all that important. However, the Bible tells us that it should be studied and read by large groups, families, and individuals.

The Bible demonstrates that it is to be read and studied in groups. Moses spoke and read the words of God to the Israelites as they camped at Mount Sinai (Exodus 24:3–8). God commanded through Moses that the law should be read to all the people in Israel, even visitors, during a festival that was to be held every seven years (Deuteronomy 31:9–13). One of the first things Joshua did after entering the Promised Land was fulfill God's order to have all the people stand near two mountains and read the law, both the blessings for obedience and the curses for disobedience (Joshua 8:33–35). After the people returned from captivity in Babylon and Persia, Ezra the priest read the law to everyone who was present in Jerusalem (Nehemiah 8:1–3). Paul referred to the scriptures being read in the synagogues every Sabbath (Acts 13:27). As a conclusion of the Council of Jerusalem, James testified that the scriptures, especially those written by Moses, were read every Sabbath in the synagogues all around the world (Acts 15:21). We have already discussed how the Bible is a pillar of the church. However, the Bible does not stop there in its desire to communicate with people.

It is also important for families to study the scriptures together. The Bible demonstrates that it is meant to be used by families. Moses reminded the people that God wants them to teach their children about the scriptures (Deuteronomy 4:7–10). The scriptures were to be such a part of family life that everything the family did would teach the children how to live for God (Deuteronomy 6:6–9, 11:18–21). Joshua commanded the people to teach their children about the miraculous crossing of the Jordan River (Joshua 4:4–7).

Just as the Bible is a pillar in the life of the church, it is also a pillar in an individual's relationship with God. Psalm 1 extols the benefits of knowing and delighting in the law of God. It uses singular pronouns to show that it is directed at individuals. Verse 2 tells us that the righteous person delights in the law of God while the ungodly person does not. Scripture delights the individual person, not just in the reading of it, but in the obeying of it. The individual seeks wisdom, strength, and solace from the words of God. To refuse to make the scriptures personal, or to refuse to study them in a personal way is to deprive your spirit of growth and happiness.

Other passages also show us that the Bible is for individuals. Joshua followed Moses as the leader of Israel. He led the people into the Promised Land and conquered the territory. Before Joshua gave his first official order, God spoke with him. In Joshua 1:7–8, God told Joshua to observe the law that had been given through Moses and to meditate on it day and night. The law was to be a part of Joshua's life every time he made a decision. It was to be personal to him.

God believed it was important for the future kings of Israel to read the scriptures. He commanded that they make a copy of the scriptures and read and study it all the days of their lives (Deuteronomy 17:18–19). Each king was to obey the laws of God so that he would live in close relationship with God and serve as an example to the people to do the same. By following the laws of God, the king could ensure that the people were being treated fairly. It was important that this individual study the scriptures to lead the rest of Israel into personal study and living according to God's word.

Psalm 119 is an ode to the word of God. It extols the benefits of the individual who observes the moral life God set out through scripture. Blessed is the person who keeps the word of God (verse 1). The way to maintain or return to moral purity is to follow the rules set by God in scripture (verse 9). It is obvious that the writer took this personally as singular pronouns are used throughout the psalm.

It is important that we understand that the scriptures are for individuals and not just for large groups. This concept helps us to correctly identify God as a personal God, not just a God of the masses. God is concerned about us as individuals. Jesus told us that God knows when a sparrow falls, yet we are more important than a sparrow. He also said that God knows us so intimately that the hairs on our head are numbered (Matthew 10:29–31). Finally, he made it a point to speak to individuals, not just large groups. God is concerned about the individual and has structured the message of the scriptures in a way that speaks to individuals.

It's All about You

You might be wondering how all of the ground we have covered in this book applies to you as an individual. It is easy to see how all of this can apply to the global church and multiple communities and cultures, but the real question is how it connects with you.

One of the things I stressed in this book is that we are not in the middle of a new time of silence from God. God is constantly and consistently speaking to individuals through the scriptures and the Holy Spirit. God is not merely concerned with the group called the church; God's concern centers around the individuals who make up that group and extends beyond it to those who are not yet members.

Not knowing the past places a road block in front of the message God gives through the writer. We must also remember that it helps to know some of the history of the writer in order to understand what they are communicating to the receptor. All of the biblical writers shared the history found in the Bible. It is their history of their people.

We discussed that special revelation, the Bible, is one of the factors that provides the boundaries for our interpretations of the scriptures. Scripture interprets scripture. Therefore, the more familiar a person is with the biblical story, the better that person will be able to properly interpret what is found in the Bible. The more of the Bible you know, the less chance there is you will make an error when finding the meaning of a passage.

We then turned our attention to how communication works. Individuals are consistent in the way they communicate with each other, even though there are varying methods. We all need the same basic information to understand what is being communicated by another person. These basic rules are true for every language and culture.

We found that God used the rules and confines of human communication to reach us with his message. It would have been easy for God to use some form of communication that was foreign to humans and then make it understandable only to a select few. But God had you in mind when he first gave the message to the biblical writers. God knew how you would communicate and understand, and followed the rules in order to reach you with the message.

God did not use just one method, i.e., written communication. He used multiple formats so he could reach more individuals. You may like reading historical stories, or poetry, or legal code, or letters with well-considered arguments. No matter which type excites you and helps you to connect with and understand his message, the Bible has it. This is another example of the detail God placed into the Bible to reach individuals like you and me.

God used the common language of the people to communicate the message. He wanted as many people as possible to find meaning from it. That is why he used Hebrew, Aramaic, and Greek as the original languages of the Bible.

Translations continued God's initial program of communicating in the language of the people. As Christianity spread, people translated the Bible into their own languages. Syriac, Latin, Coptic, Chinese, and eventually English were just a few of the languages the Bible was translated into with the goal of expanding the message to new people. Today, many people are translating the Bible into even more languages. This effort is led by the Holy Spirit, as God wants every individual to read the message of the Bible for himself in a language he can understand. It is exciting to know that God has provided a translation of the Bible in my language. It makes me feel that God is concerned about those who are in my group, and also that he wants to speak to me directly. I hope you get that feeling as well as you read through your translation of the Bible.

Our discussion of the Bible's cross-cultural properties, and the fact that God designed the it to be cross-cultural, convinced me that God wanted the Bible to reach me directly, in the culture in which I live. In other words, God consciously made the Bible cross-cultural so you could identify the message with your culture and in your time and place. This was a deliberate act of love by God.

Think about the thought and care God took in ensuring the Bible would be relevant to both oral and written traditions. Israel was mostly an oral tradition culture at the time, with a few who could read a written language. From the time of Moses to the New Testament era, most cultures remained in this cross-over period between oral and written. Today, while many people live in cultures dominated by the written word, there are still some who use oral methods for learning. No matter which culture you live in, God wants to speak to you.

The global church provides culturally diverse interpretations while creating boundaries for interpretation. This is true for the historical as well as the contemporary church. Each member of a congregation learns these boundaries, which help during personal times of learning about the Bible. Most of us are content with the boundaries formed by our congregations, but some will seek to find out what conclusions other congregations have come to about God's message. I really became interested in this topic by reading works by people like Justo Gonzalez, Simon Chan, Cain Hope Felder, and others, who stayed within the boundaries of communication but were able to see things through their own cultures.

It is through the church that cultures can contribute to the interpretation of scripture. In other words, your culture has something to offer regarding the interpretation of the Bible. Concerning the Latino viewpoint, Justo Gonzalez says, "If it is true that we bring a particular perspective to history and to theology, then we must also bring a particular perspective to the interpretation of Scripture. And, once again, it may be that this perspective will prove useful not only to us but also to the church at large."[96] The church cannot afford to discount anyone's interpretation of scripture. God can speak to and through any culture. Your cultural insights into the interpretation of the Bible may also be valuable to your neighbor and to the world. That is a powerful thought. The concept of the transcultural church interpreting the Bible through transcultural eyes brings a richer, fuller meaning to the message God has given to humans. You, as an individual, are a part of that as you take what God says to you through the Bible and share it with others.

It is amazing to me the pains God took to communicate with individuals. God put so much creativity and attention to detail in how the message was presented because God had you in mind when he wrote it. As we look at the Bible, we find that God spoke to groups through individuals. The message of the Bible is an individual one that touches each person where he or she needs it most, whether it is a need for correction or comfort. By using true, historical stories of real people, God shows us that he is concerned with real life, not just theories. The real-life message is meant to touch your life, where you live. God used common rules of language in order to reach the average individual. He used a cross-cultural format to reach all cultures. His desire for relationship with you spurred him to create a form of communication that would reach you personally. There is no doubt in my mind that the Bible is an act of love by God to each individual in every culture, especially you.

Notes

1. Webster's New World Dictionary: Third College Edition, 1988.
2. Donald K. Smith, *Creating Understanding: A Handbook for Christian Communications Across Cultural Landscapes* (Grand Rapids, MI: Zondervan Publishing House), pp. 78, 112–13.
3. Virgilio Elizondo, *Galilean Journey: The Mexican-American Promise* (Maryknoll, NY: Orbis Books, 2009), p.51.
4. Smith, *Creating Understanding*, p. 78.
5. Smith, *Creating Understanding*, p. 78.
6. Herodotus, Book 2, paragraphs 36, 37, 104.
7. Herodotus, Book 2, paragraph 37
8. Herodotus, Book 2, paragraph 37
9. Herodotus, Book 2, paragraph 37
10. Herodotus, Book 2, paragraph 38
11. Willis Judson Beecher, D.D., *The Prophets and the Promise: Being for Substance: The Lectures for 1902–1903 on the L. P. Stone Foundation in the Princeton Theological Seminary* (Eugene, OR: Wipf and Stock Publishers, 2002), pp. 263–88.
12. Beecher, *The Prophets and the Promise*, p. 265.
13. Beecher, *The Prophets and the Promise*, p. 279.
14. Beecher, *The Prophets and the Promise*, p. 275.
15. Beecher, *The Prophets and the Promise*, pp. 289–312.
16. Beecher, *The Prophets and the Promise*, pp. 313–29.
17. Beecher, *The Prophets and the Promise*, p. 313.

18. Gerald O'Collins, *Christology: A Biblical, Historical, and Systematic Study of Jesus* (Oxford, New York: Oxford University Press, 2009), p. 143.

19. Nancy L. Eisland, *The Disabled God: Toward a Liberation Theology of Disability* (Nashville, TN: Abingdon Press, 1994).

20. Justo L. Gonzalez, *Mañana: Christian Theology from a Hispanic Perspective* (Nashville, TN: Abingdon Press, 1990).

21. Elizondo, *Galilean Journey: The Mexican-American Promise*, p.51.

22. Volker Küster, *The Many Faces of Jesus Christ* (Maryknoll, NY: Orbis Books, 2001).

23. Smith, *Creating Understanding*, p. 185.

24. Jeannine K. Brown, *Introducing Biblical Hermeneutics: Scripture As Communication* (Grand Rapids, MI: Baker Academic, 2007), p. 140.

25. Brown, *Introducing Biblical Hermeneutics*, p. 148.

26. Brown, *Introducing Biblical Hermeneutics*, p. 150.

27. Brown, *Introducing Biblical Hermeneutics*, p. 157.

28. Smith, *Creating Understanding*, p. 113.

29. Smith, *Creating Understanding*, p. 113.

30. Jacob Neusner, "Introduction," in *Babylonian Talmud, Volume 1*, ed. Jacob Neusner (Peabody, MA: Hendrickson Publishers), p. xxviii.

31. Josephus, *Antiquities*, 14.7.2. The temple in Jerusalem had been rebuilt when the people returned from Persia.

32. Josephus, *Antiquities*, 12.3.1.

33. A. Cleveland Coxe, "Introductory Note," in *Ante-Nicene Fathers*, volume 3, ed. Alexander Roberts and James Donaldson (Peabody, MA: Hendrickson Publishers), p. 3.

34. Philip Jenkins, *The Lost History of Christianity: The Thousand-Year Golden Age of the Church of the Middle East, Africa, and Asia—and How It Died* (New York: Harper One), p. 6.

35. Samuel Hugh Moffet, *A History of Christianity in Asia, Volume I: Beginnings to 1500* (Maryknoll, New York: Orbis Books, 1998), p. 266.

36. Moffet, *A History of Christianity in Asia*, p. 208.

37. Moffet, *A History of Christianity in Asia*, p. 257.

38. Moffet, *A History of Christianity in Asia*, p. 293.

39. Gonzalez, *Mañana*, p. 84.

40. Jenkins, *The Lost History of Christianity*, p. 39.

41. Sir Lancelot C. L. Brenton, "Introduction," in *The Septuagint with Apocrypha: Greek and English* (Peabody, MA: Hendrickson Publishers), p. ii.

42. Jenkins, *The Lost History of Christianity*, p. 77.

43. Charles H. Kraft, *Communication Theory for Christian Witness*, rev. ed. (Maryknoll, NY: Orbis Books, 1991), p. 49.

44. Jenkins, *The Lost History of Christianity*, p. 77.

45. Moffet, *A History of Christianity in Asia*, p. 74.

46. Moffet, *A History of Christianity in Asia*, p. 206.

47. Moffet, *A History of Christianity in Asia*, p. 74

48. Jenkins, *The Lost History of Christianity*, p. 77.

49. Jenkins, *The Lost History of Christianity*, pp. 62–63.

50. Moffet, *A History of Christianity in Asia*, pp. 300–301.

51. Kraft, *Communication Theory*, p. 128.

52. Translators to the Readers 1611 KJV.

53. Kraft, *Communication Theory*, p. 32.

54. Moffet, *A History of Christianity in Asia*, 329–32.

55. Kraft, *Communication Theory*, p. 48.

56. Moffet, *A History of Christianity in Asia*, p. 332.

57. Kraft, *Communication Theory*, p. 96.

58. Webster's New World Dictionary, p. xix.

59. Webster's New World Dictionary, p. xix.

60. Webster's New World Dictionary, p. xxii.

61. Webster's New World Dictionary, p. xxii.

62. Smith, *Creating Understanding*, p. 56.

63. Smith, *Creating Understanding*, p. 57.

64. Smith, *Creating Understanding*, p. 185.

65. Smith, *Creating Understanding*, p. 200.

66. Gonzalez, *Mañana*, pp. 44–45.

67. Stephanie Buckhanon Crowder, "The Gospel of Luke," in *Stony the Road We Trod: African American Biblical Interpretation*, ed. Cain Hope Felder (Minneapolis: Fortress Press, 1991), pp. 174–75.

68. Paul John Isaak, "Luke," in *Africa Bible Commentary*, ed. Tokunboh Adeyemo (Nairobi, Kenya: Word Alive Publishers, 2006), 1233–237.

69. Smith, *Creating Understanding*, p. 241.

70. Kraft, *Communication Theory*, p. 15.

71. Kraft, *Communication Theory*, p. 16.

72. Kraft, *Communication Theory*, p. 15.

73. Kraft, *Communication Theory*, p. 14.

74. Francis A. Schaeffer, *The Francis A. Schaeffer Trilogy: He Is There and He Is Not Silent* (Westchester, IL: Crossway Books, 1990), p. 325.

75. Kraft, *Communication Theory*, p. 14.

76. Kraft, *Communication Theory*, p. 20.

77. James B. Pritchard, ed., *Ancient Near Eastern Texts Relating to the Old Testament*, 3rd ed. with suppl. (Princeton, NJ: Princeton University Press, 1969), p. 326.

78. Webster's New World Dictionary.

79. Cain Hope Felder, "Introduction," in *Stony the Road We Trod: African American Biblical Interpretation*, ed. Cain Hope Felder (Minneapolis: Fortress Press, 1991), p. 6.

80. Mark L. Y. Chan, "Hermeneutics," in *Global Dictionary of Theology*, eds. William A. Dyrness, and Veli-Matti Kärkkäinen (Downers Grove, IL: InterVarsity Press, 2008), p. 380.

81. William H. Meyers, "The Hermeneutical Dilemma," in *Stony the Road We Trod: African American Biblical Interpretation*, ed. Cain Hope Felder (Minneapolis: Fortress Press, 1991), p. 46.

82. Meyers, "The Hermeneutical Dilemma," p. 42.

83. Kraft, *Communication Theory*, p. 96.

84. Meyers, "The Hermeneutical Dilemma," p. 46.

85. Kwame Bediako, "Scripture as the Interpreter of Culture and Tradition," in *Africa Bible Commentary*. ed. Tokunboh Adeyemo (Nairobi, Kenya: Word Alive Publishers, 2006), p. 3.

86. Justo L. Gonzalez, *Santa Biblia: The Bible Through Hispanic Eyes* (Nashville, TN: Abingdon Press, 1996), p. 118.

87. Gonzalez, *Santa Biblia*, p. 115.

88. Gonzalez, *Santa Biblia*, p. 116.

89. Gonzalez, *Santa Biblia*, p. 117.

90. Clement of Alexandria, *The Stromata, or Miscellanies*, Book 7, chap. 16.

91. Clement of Alexandria, *The Stromata, or Miscellanies*, Book 7, chap. 16.

92. Justin Martyr, *Dialogue With Trypho*, chap. 68.

93. *The Canons of the Blessed and Holy Fathers Assembled at Antioch in Syria*, Canon 2 (341 CE).

94. Moffet, *A History of Christianity in Asia*, p. 312.

95. Elizabeth Conde-Frazier, S. Steve Kang, and Gary A. Parrett, *A Many Colored Kingdom: Multicultural Dynamics for Spiritual Formation* (Grand Rapids, MI: Baker Academic), p. 13.

96. Gonzalez, *Mañana*, p. 75.

GLOSSARY

allowable meaning: Shades of understanding that are close enough for the two parties to agree that communication has been achieved.

church: In this book, "the church" means the global church, all Christians currently living. It can also refer to a local congregation.

communication: Can be described as one person trying to express his thoughts to another.

communicator: The one who is expressing his thoughts.

context: (1) The words and paragraphs around a certain part of writing; (2) the situation a person is in at a specific time, for example, at the moment he is communicating about something.

cross-cultural: Related to more than one culture.

cultural sensitivity: Tailoring communication to help someone from another culture understand what is being said.

culture: The ideas, customs, skills, arts, etc., of a people or group, which are transferred, communicated, or passed along to succeeding generations.

diversity: In the context of the church, the ability to have multiple cultures represented within a congregation, with each culture being treated equally.

general revelation: God speaking through creation.

genre: The types of communication used, generally identified with writing.

hermeneutics: According to Webster's dictionary, "the art or science of the interpretation of literature."

illumination: Part of relational revelation; the Holy Spirit helps people understand specific revelation, but does not reveal anything new.

interpretation: How we understand what someone else means when he tries to communicate.

mission: Carrying God's message to other people.

receptor: Also known as the receiver, the receptor attempts to make sense of what is expressed.

relational revelation: What we find when we see Jesus communicating with people, or the Holy Spirit living within Christians and guiding them in the truth.

revelation (to reveal): To present that which was hidden, to present something new to a receptor.

specific revelation: This occurs when God speaks to humans directly, as he did to the Bible authors.

stew of meaning: Theory that states meaning is like a stew to which the communicator and the receptor each add their ingredients.

transcultural: The ability to go beyond culture and relate at a level that is common to all humans.

translation: Taking communication from one language and placing it in another.

BIBLIOGRAPHY

Adeyemo, Tokunboh, ed. *Africa Bible Commentary*. Nairobi, Kenya: Word Alive Publishers, 2006.

Beecher, Willis Judson. *The Prophets and the Promise: Being for Substance; The Lectures for 1902–1903; On the L. P. Stone Foundation in the Princeton Theological Seminary*. Eugene, OR: Wipf and Stock Publishers, 2002.

Brenton, Sir Lancelot C. L. *The Septuagint with Apocrypha: Greek and English*. Peabody, MA: Hendrickson Publishers, 1986.

Brown, Jeannine K. *Scripture as Communication: Introducing Biblical Hermeneutics*. Grand Rapids, MI: Baker Academic, 2007.

Conde-Frazier, Elizabeth, S. Steve Kang, and Garry A. Parrett. *A Many Colored Kingdom: Multicultural Dynamics for Spiritual Formation*. Grand Rapids, MI: Baker Academic, 2004.

Dyrness, William A., and Veli-Matti Kärkkäinen, eds. *Global Dictionary of Theology*. Downers Grove, IL: InterVarsity Press. 2008.

Eiesland, Nancy L. *The Disabled God: Toward a Liberatory Theology of Disability*. Nashville, TN: Abingdon Press, 1994.

Elizondo, Virgilio. *Galilean Journey: The Mexican-American Promise*. Maryknoll, NY: Orbis Books, 2009.

Felder, Cain Hope, ed. *Stony the Road We Trod: African American Biblical Interpretation.* Minneapolis: Fortress Press, 1991.

Gonzalez, Justo L. *Santa Biblia: The Bible Through Hispanic Eyes.* Nashville, TN: Abingdon Press, 1996.

———. *Mañana: Christian Theology from a Hispanic Perspective.* Nashville, TN: Abingdon Press, 1990.

Jenkins, Philip. *The Lost History of Christianity: The Thousand-Year Golden Age of the Church in the Middle East, Africa, and Asia—and How It Died.* New York: HarperOne, 2008.

Kraft, Charles H. *Communication Theory for Christian Witness.* Rev. ed. Maryknoll, NY: Orbis Books, 1991.

Küster, Volker. *The Many Faces of Jesus Christ: Intercultural Christology.* Maryknoll, NY: Orbis Books, 2001.

McDowell, Josh. *Evidence That Demands a Verdict: Historical Evidences for the Christian Faith*, vol. 1. San Bernardino, CA: Here's Life Publishers, 1991.

Moffet, Samuel Hugh. *A History of Christianity in Asia, Volume I: Beginnings to 1500.* Maryknoll, NY: Orbis Books, 1998.

Neusner, Jacob. *The Babylonian Talmud: A Translation and Commentary, Volume 1, Tractate Berakhot.* Peabody, MA: Hendrickson Publishers Marketing, 2005.

O'Collins, Gerald. *Christology: A Biblical, Historical, and Systematic Study of Jesus.* 2nd ed. Oxford: Oxford University Press, 2009.

Pritchard, James B., ed. *Ancient Near Eastern Texts Relating to the Old Testament.* 3rd ed. with supplement. Princeton, NJ: Princeton University Press, 1969.

Roberts, Alexander, and James Donaldson, eds. *The Writings of the Fathers Down to A.D. 325: Ante-Nicene Fathers, Volume 3: Latin Christianity: Its Founder, Tertullian: I. Apologetic; II. Anti-Marcion; III. Ethical.* Peabody, MA: Hendrickson Publishers Marketing, 2012.

Schaeffer, Francis A. *The Francis A. Schaeffer Trilogy: The Three Essential Books in One Volume; Book Three; He Is There and He Is Not Silent.* Westchester, IL: Crossway Books, 1990.

Smith, Donald K. *Creating Understanding: A Handbook for Christian Communication across Cultural Landscapes.* Grand Rapids, MI: Zondervan Publishing House, 1992.

INDEX

general revelation and, 44
identification with Bible
characters, 65
Jesus and religious leaders,
74–76
love of God, 81–82
questions to discern meaning,
35
Scripture, 98–99
the Temptation, 70
and the term "Lord," 16
Ptolemy Philadelphus, 23

R

ra'ah, 12
Rabbula, 24
receptor, 110
receptor oriented communication,
46
Red Sea, 36
Reformation, 56
relational revelation, 45, 52, 58,
110
religious laws, 13–14, 49–51,
80–81
revelation
agreement of, 46, 58
as communication, 43, 44
defined, 110
general, 44–45, 58, 110
Holy Spirit and, 45, 46, 52
knowing and, 43
language of, 46–49
laws and rituals, 49–51
nature and, 44
relational, 45, 52, 58, 110
specific, 45, 53, 58, 110
truth and, 46, 47
Revelation, book of, 11

revenge, 72
rituals, 49–51
Roman Catholic Church. *See*
Catholic Church
Romans, 44
Rome, 21
Ruth, book of, 12

S

sacrifices, animal, 14, 50
Sadducees, 75
salvation, 13
Saul, 6
Schaeffer, Francis, 49
School of Alexandria, 21
Scripture. *See* Bible
Septuagint, 23–24
Sermon on the Mount, 70–72
Servant, 10, 15
Shakespeare, William, 35
Simeon, 10
Smith, Donald K., xiv, 13, 17, 18,
38–40, 45
Solomon, 5, 6
special servant. *See* Servant
specific revelation, 45, 53, 58, 110
Stephen (the martyr), 90
stew of meaning, 37–42, 52, 57,
59, 110
stories, 17–18, 65
synagogues, 20, 22
Syriac language, 24

T

tabernacles, 12
Tatian, 21, 24
temples, 12
The Temptation, 69–70
Ten Commandments, 71–72

Tennessee Temple University, xiv
Theophilus of Antioch, 21
Thomas, 22
Timothy, 45, 60, 88
transcultural, 110
transcultural hermeneutic, 56, 59,
    63–67, 79–83
translations, 23–26, 100, 110
truth, 46, 47
Trypho, 88

U
Uriah, 40

V
values, 32–33, 34, 51
Vulgate, 24, 25

W
Webster's Dictionary, 37–38
Wycliffe, John, 25